ARCHITECTURAL DESIGN

EDITORIAL OFFICES:
42 LEINSTER GARDENS, LONDON W2 3AN
TEL: 0171-402 2141 FAX: 0171-723 9540

EDITOR: Maggie Toy
EDITORIAL TEAM: Stephen Watt, Ramona Khambatta
ART EDITOR: Andrea Bettella
CHIEF DESIGNER: Mario Bettella
DESIGNER: Gregory Mills

CONSULTANTS: Catherine Cooke, Terry Farrell, Kenneth Frampton, Charles Jencks, Heinrich Klotz, Leon Krier, Robert Maxwell, Demetri Porphyrios, Kenneth Powell, Colin Rowe, Derek Walker

SUBSCRIPTION OFFICES:
UK: ACADEMY GROUP LTD
42 LEINSTER GARDENS
LONDON W2 3AN
TEL: 0171-402 2141 FAX: 0171-723 9540

USA AND CANADA: VCH PUBLISHERS NEW YORK INC, SUITE 907, 220 EAST 23RD STREET NEW YORK, NY 10010-4606
TEL: (212) 683 8333 FAX: (212) 779 8890

ALL OTHER COUNTRIES:
VCH VERLAGSGESELLSCHAFT MBH
BOSCHSTRASSE 12, POSTFACH 101161
69451 WEINHEIM
FEDERAL REPUBLIC OF GERMANY
TEL: +49 6201 606 148 FAX: +49 6201 606 184

© 1996 Academy Group Ltd. All rights reserved. No part of this publication may be reproduced or transmitted in any form or by any means, electronic or mechanical, including photocopying, recording or any information storage or retrieval system without permission in writing from the Publishers. Neither the Editor nor the Academy Group hold themselves responsible for the opinions expressed by writers of articles or letters in this magazine. The Editor will give careful consideration to unsolicited articles, photographs and drawings; please enclose a stamped addressed envelope for their return (if required). Payment for material appearing in AD is not normally made except by prior arrangement. All reasonable care will be taken of material in the possession of AD and agents and printers, but they regret that they cannot be held responsible for any loss or damage.

Architectural Design is published six times per year (Jan/Feb; Mar/Apr; May/Jun; Jul/Aug; Sept/Oct; and Nov/Dec). Subscription rates for 1996 (incl p&p): Annual subscription price: UK only £68.00, World DM 195, USA $142.00 for regular subscribers. Student rate: UK only £50.00, World DM 156, USA $105.00 incl postage and handling charges. Individual issues: £16.95/DM 42.50 (plus £2.40/DM 6 for p&p, per issue ordered), US $28.95 (incl p&p).
For the USA and Canada, Architectural Design is distributed by VCH Publishers New York Inc, Suite 907, 220 East 23rd Street New York, NY 10010-4606; Tel: (212) 683 8333, Fax: (212) 779 8890. Application to mail at second-class postage rates is pending at New York, NY. POSTMASTER. Send address changes to Architectural Design, VCH Publishers New York Inc, Suite 907, 220 East 23rd Street, New York, NY 10010-4606. Printed in Italy. Origination by Media 2000, London.
All prices are subject to change without notice. [ISSN: 0003-8504]

R0693

KU-474-882

CONTENTS

ARCHITECTURAL DESIGN MAGAZINE

Battle McCarthy *Multi-Source Synthesis: An Architecture of Smell* • **Christian Brensing** *Berlin: Young Architects Today* • *Academy Highlights* • *Books* • *Exhibitions*

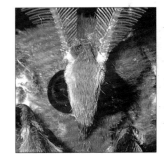

The most acute sense of smell exhibited in nature is that of the male emperor moth

ARCHITECTURAL DESIGN PROFILE No 121

GAMES OF ARCHITECTURE

James Williamson *Acupuncture* • **Baratloo and Balch** *Angst Cartography* • **Chora/Raoul Bunschoten** *Arabianranta* • **Paul Edwards/Ou. Pho. Po.** *Bruges-La-Morte* • **Jae-Eun Choi** *Chaos* • **Joan Fontcuberta** *Compared Anatomy* • **Stan Allen** *Field Conditions* • **Arakawa and Gins** *Gifu – Reversible Destiny* • **Jennifer Bloomer** *Hypertextual Picturesque* • **Frank Gehry/Philip Johnson** *Lewis House* • **a. topos** *Light ness* • **OMA: Rem Koolhaas/ Bruce Mau** *Negotiation* • **Preston Scott Cohen** *Stereotomic Permutations* • **Vito Acconci/Steven Holl** *Storefront* • **Armand Schwerner** *Tablets*

Huber and Staudt, loft conversion, Schinke Straße, Berlin

Chora/Raoul Bunschoten, game board, Helsinki, Arabianranta

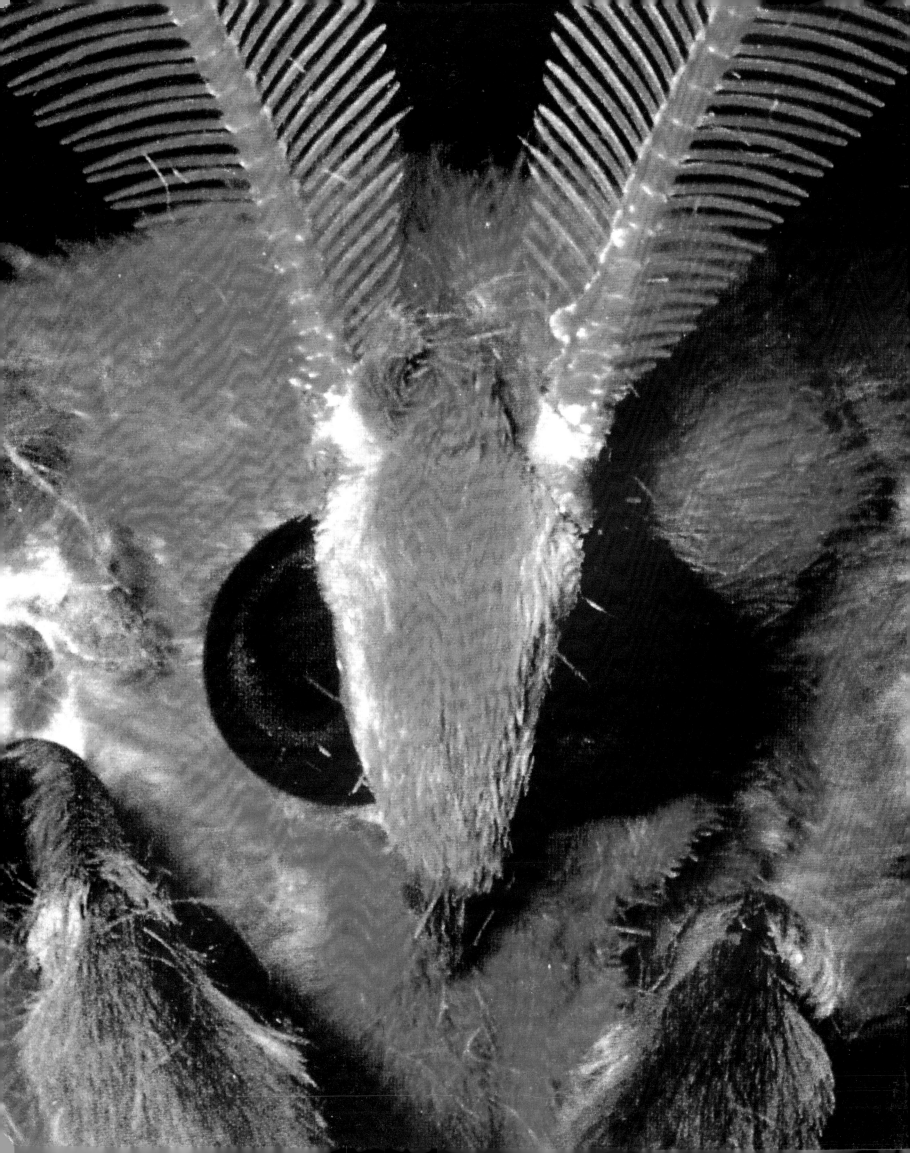

BATTLE McCARTHY
MULTI-SOURCE SYNTHESIS
An Architecture of Smell

Smells and tastes . . . alone, more fragile but more enduring, more insubstantial, more persistent . . . bear unflinchingly, in the tiny and almost impalpable drop of their essence, the vast structure of recollection.
Marcel Proust, *Remembrance of Things Past*

And so he would now study perfumes . . . He saw that there was no mood of the mind that had not its counterpart in the sensuous life, and set himself to discover their true relations, wondering what there was in frankincense that made one mystical, and in ambergris that stirred one's passions, and in violets that woke the memory of dead romances, and in musk that troubled the brain, and in champak that stained the imagination; and seeking often to elaborate a real psychology of perfumes, and to estimate the several influences of sweet-smelling roots, and scented pollen-laden flowers, or aromatic balms, and of dark and fragrant woods, of spikenard that sickens, of hovenia that makes men mad, and of aloes that are said to be able to expel melancholy from the soul.
Oscar Wilde, *The Picture of Dorian Gray*

Smells and fragrances have always played a critical role in human affairs but, of all the senses, smell is the least researched and understood. In fact, over the last 2,000 years, its perceived importance has been gradually undermined by a combination of cultural conceit and odour pollution.

But smell is undergoing a renaissance. Engineers are relatively skilled in the design of visual and acoustic environments, even if only to satisfy functional requirements. However, designers are now creating olfactory environments; places where smell is used to create emotion, recollection and mood.

Smell is arguably the most subtle and powerful sense in its potential for emotional impact. Humans can recognise 10,000 different odours, each of which has distinct characteristics and associations for each individual. Smells can induce fear, desire or joy, defining our experience of space in often unconscious ways.

The science of smell
Odour is our response to molecular compounds of varying size and structure. The smell receptors are tiny hairs, or cilia, on neurones located in the olfactory epithelium of the nasal cavity. These neurones are the only direct physical connection between the external world and the brain as they are in constant contact with inhaled air. Odour molecules bind to receptor proteins on the cilia which stimulate a tiny electrical charge along axons to the olfactory bulbs in the brain.

Each odour consists of a mixture of many different chemicals, though the perception is of one distinct smell rather than a series of individual components. Different neurones respond to different chemicals, so that each odour has its own pattern of responding neurones; forming a particular image inside the brain.

The psychology of smell is extremely complex as odours are processed in the part of the brain concerned with emotional response. Hence, individuals respond differently to the same odours, with sensitivity varying with time and age, as well as mood. Similarly women are more sensitive to smells than men and certain people are able to ignore particular odours after prolonged exposure.

The impact of smells can be directly measured by recording electrical activity in the brain in relation to exposure. Upward shifts in brain-wave activity have been measured after exposure to jasmine or peppermint oil, indicating a stimulating effect, whilst oils such as lavender or sandalwood produce a downward shift, indicating a sedative effect. Research in this area is still in its early stages, though it promises to map one of the most unexplored areas of human knowledge.

Towards an architecture of smell
Current attempts to use smell in architecture are crude and usually focused on the single goal of selling; supermarkets pumping the smell of freshly baked bread into their lobbies to lure customers in. However, there are a few examples of more inventive application. In Japan, firms are using fragrance to increase worker productivity, using a variety of odours throughout the day. Citrus and peppermint smells are used to counteract early morning or afternoon fatigue, and wood smells are used at lunch to underline the fact that it is time to rest.

Smells can be used to construct a physical

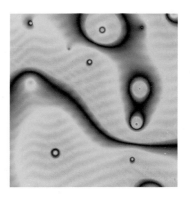

OPPOSITE: The most acute sense of smell exhibited in nature is that of the male emperor moth (Eudia Pavonia) which, according to German experiments carried out in 1961, can detect the sex attractant of the virgin female at a range of 11km upwind. The scent has been identified as one of the higher alcohols ($C_{16}H_{29}OH$), of which the female carries less than 0.0001mg; ABOVE: Computer visualisation of scent contours diffusing through space.

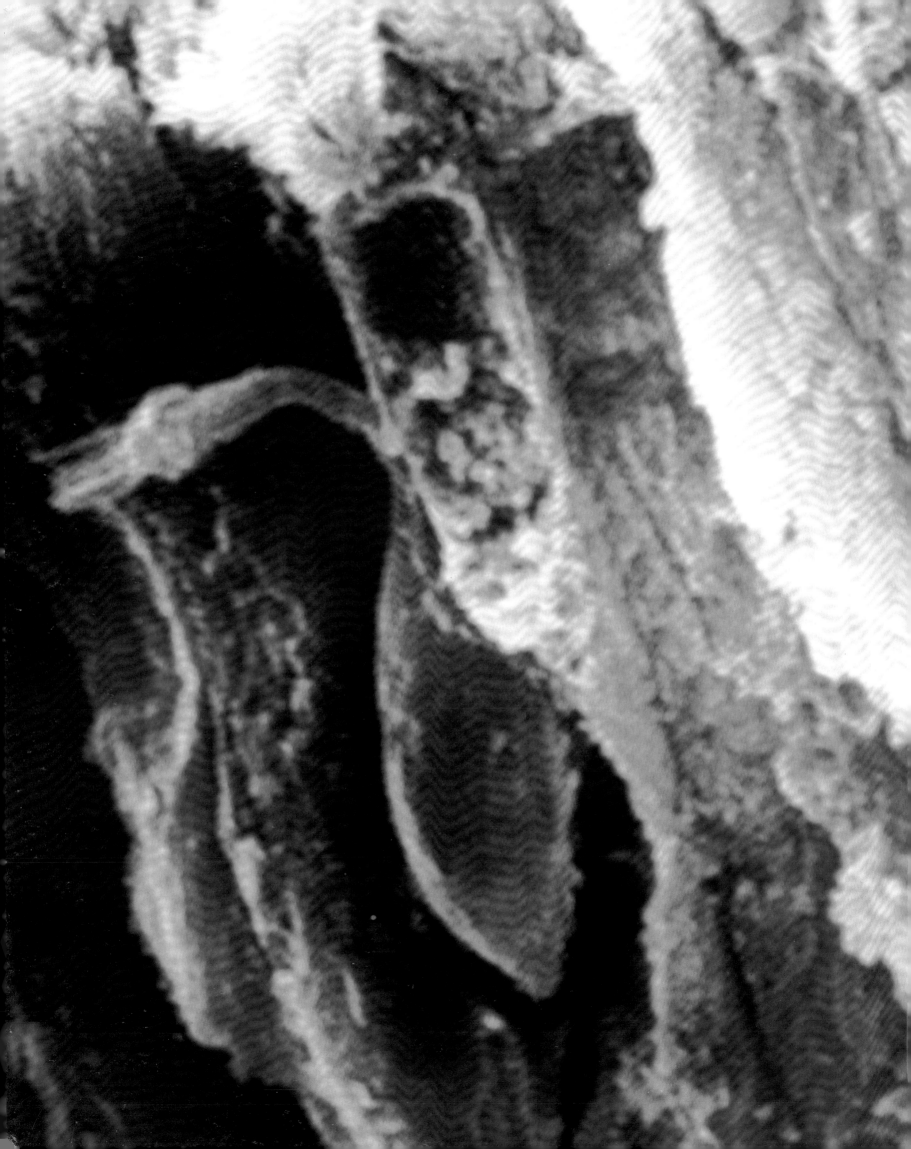

architecture in the same way that light and sound can be used to sculpt or define space. Smells can form olfactory barriers – working like mosquito repellents – or tempting trails. One of the most famous odour experiments involves pheromones (human sexual scents). Women or men entering a waiting-room have been observed to repeatedly choose to sit in the chair that has been sprayed with the pheromone of the opposite sex, even when all others remain unoccupied.

Public spaces should have a celebratory architecture of smell. Temples and churches still use fragrance to lift the spirit and transform the everyday, while modern secular spaces have opted for a democratic blandness. Instead they should be vibrant and replete with scent. In the past this was woven into the fabric of the building itself to ensure an aromatic atmosphere; early Indian temples were constructed entirely from sandalwood, and to the mortar of their temples the Babylonians added perfume. Today, modern approaches are more likely to be software-based, with air handling systems and dedicated equipment generating and distributing smell.

Using software-based odour generation, public spaces could be filled with constantly varying olfactory environments, ebbing and flowing in response to the season, time of day or weather, or to any other combination of variables; the actions and movements of visitors; the inputs of a million people via the internet, or a model of the world stock market.

Design with odour
Although humans can distinguish between many thousands of different odours, they lack the appropriate vocabulary to describe or draw them, hindering attempts to integrate olfaction into the design process. Wine-tasters and other odour professionals have had to define their own language, and the unit of smell, the Olf, can only be defined by experts specially trained for the purpose. In Scandinavia 'Sensory Panels' are employed by the government to monitor the air quality standard in buildings by carrying out olfactory inspections of the interior spaces on a regular basis. Eventually these smell specialists will become as vital to designers as lightmeters and thermometers.

Unfortunately these methods are devised with the intention of analysing existing odours rather than producing an aromatic palette. Instead, it seems likely that a system of colour-coded analysis – used today for the representation of light and sound – will be developed enabling designers to create and communicate proposals for specific olfactory environments. The designer will be able to select from an infinite range of smells randomly generated by computer, and evolve new combinations of scents by the mixing and mating of components. Other methods will rely on more intuitive and evolutionary techniques.

The use of aromatic herbs and essential oils dates back to the early days of civilisation. Smells have been used as anti-depressants, euphorics, sedatives, aphrodisiacs and more, but the future of olfactory architecture will surpass these definitions. We do not know how many smells remain to be discovered.

The authors would like to thank Karin Galster and Robert Webb for their assistance with the preparation of this article.

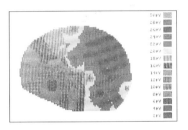

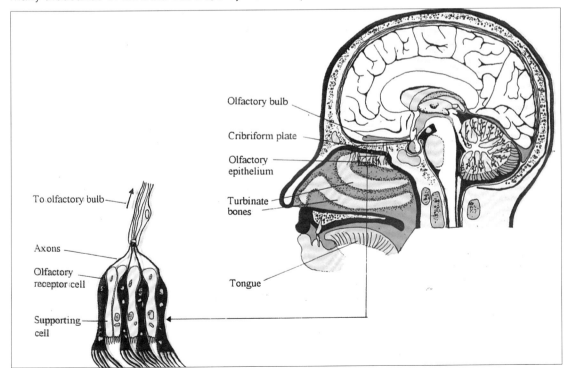

OPPOSITE: A sensory neuron in the human olfactory epithelium, surrounded by support cells. The hair-like cilia which carry the receptors can be seen protruding from its tip; FROM ABOVE: The physiology of smell; graph of recorded shifts in brainwave patterns in response to certain essential oils; BEAM scan of the brain responding to a smell identified as pleasant – the right hemisphere showing increased electrical activity.

CHRISTIAN BRENSING
BERLIN: YOUNG ARCHITECTS TODAY

Half-time
After the fall of the Wall in 1989 Berlin has been a city in transition: from the euphoria of unification to the re-establishment of political and economic power. During this period the facts, future concepts and visionary projects for the new city have been endlessly debated and publicized; with politicians and developers only partly aware of urban design's potential to support their plans for the Berlin to come. Hence architecture's prominence in the public and political debate is more related to the manifestation of power and practical influence than to mere aesthetic considerations.

This battle for Berlin has been raging ever since compulsory building guidelines were issued by the City Building Authority, with the intention to control and direct the redevelopment of the centre; largely destroyed during and after the war. However the international architectural community has not been convinced that the current legislation – eaves restricted to a height of 22m, traditional facades of stone allowing only a certain percentage of glass, site borders not to differ from those of the historic Berlin housing block and respect for the old street plan – gives Berlin a real chance to return to its true architectural roots; something, the authorities maintain was ignored and denied during the post-war reconstruction (Scharoun) and the Internationale Bauausstellung (IBA) decades.

Rather than retracing the familiar arguments, verging on the one hand on the parochial and nationalistic and on the other the universal and international, one has to ask the question whether the fate of Berlin's architecture should be sacrificed over such opinionated attitudes? Therefore the question of a 'new' architecture should not concern itself with the well-known doyens of the 'Berlin style', namely Paul Josef Kleihues, Jürgen Sawade and Hans Kollhoff, but with a generation of young German architects in their 30s: Frank Barkow and Regine Leibinger; Steffen Lehmann; Christian Huber and Joachim Staudt; Justus Pysall and Peter Ruge; Armand Grüntuch and Almut Ernst, and Eike Becker, Georg Gewers, Oliver Kühn & Swantje Kühn.

These six practices flourish because of the perceived economic and cultural prospects for a united Berlin and Germany. Reflecting the fact that in 1989 the consensus had been that Berlin would soon re-emerge as the roaring metropolis of the 20s; validated by the daring schemes put forward for Potsdamer Platz and the world record breaking 835 submissions for the Spreebogen competition in 1993. During this period the city's appeal was further enhanced by the private sector funding available and the public commitment to improve the neglected infrastructure; especially in East Berlin where there is massive investment into housing, schools and similar public institutions.

Without exception all of these young architects worked abroad before they were enticed to Berlin after the fall of the Wall and for the past five years they have worked to establish their own practices. Hopefully within the next five years the contribution of these architects to Berlin will surpass any officially imposed restrictions and they will be judged by the merits of their work alone.

Leipziger Straße, Berlin, 1928
(photo H Hoeffke)

Steffen Lehmann: Paradise Regained

A striking feature of some of Berlin's historic architecture is a distinctive visionary streak creating a subtle harmony with nature through the quality of light, the colour and types of foliage or even the impression of the night sky: architecture perceived as nature's enlightened counterpart, where simplicity is equal to clarity of vision.

This appreciation of natural beauty and a respect for architectural tradition have always been key elements in Steffen Lehmann's designs, illustrated by a project he completed at the Architectural Association involving a studio-house for the American sculptor Richard Serra in a bleak Yorkshire dale. The scheme plays on the natural tectonic and projects almost effortlessly into the open valley, reflecting the poised stillness of Serra's sculptures.

Following graduation, work in England and Japan refined Lehmann's often sculptural approach even further and since opening his own practice in Berlin in the early 90s, his designs have developed a controlled expression devoid of grand gestures. Nature, in its seemingly effortless organization, provides a suitable role model for his architecture.

Predictably Lehmann's small factory for a German manufacturer in Hartha is a highly organized though informal microcosm. The plan reveals a functional layout, including an entrance gate, production hall and administration wing, whilst the three-dimensional studies communicate the sculptural attributes of the architectural space. These qualities are particularly evident in the series of courtyards where tree trunks alternate in a subtle interplay with the slender columns of the entrance building and the more solid piloti of the administration wing; emphasizing the play of natural light on form, colour and surface.

Whereas the Hartha project is an autonomous composition, the new commercial centre in Dresden is a response to its historic context; the neighbouring Villa Eschebach and the circular shape of Albertplatz. The rhythm of the baroque layout is respected by aligning the building with the centre of the square, the oblique nature of the axis creating a tension in the otherwise highly contextual response. A straightforward design, the desire for simplicity never turns into monotony as considerable attention is given to detail, particularly in the facade.

In contrast to this restrained exterior is Lehmann's 1995 design for a school in the Berlin suburbs at Barnetstraße. Here an exuberant sunshading device sails above the orthogonal corridors and classrooms, whose rigorous organisation is a considered response to the surrounding suburban chaos. Through this scheme Lehmann once again illustrates that art and architecture are able to converge in surreal beauty.

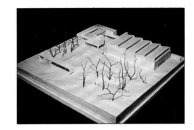

FROM ABOVE: Model; view from entrance gate; view from courtyard (factory, Hartha); BELOW, FROM LEFT: Axonometric; rendered perspective (Barnet School, Berlin)

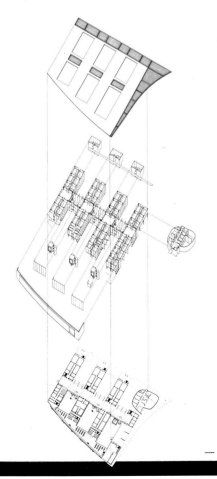

Barkow and Leibinger: Aberrant Topographies

Berlin, the largest German city, went through various phases of rapid growth until the late 30s creating numerous city centres; a disparate swirl around Potsdamer Platz, Alexander Platz and Kurfürstendamm as depicted in George Grosz's contemporaneous paintings. The war and the construction of the Wall in 1961 halted this exuberance, freezing further urban development and imposing a rigid *status quo;* embodied by the mine fields, barbed wire and concrete which encircled West Berlin.

This desolate urban periphery is the location of Frank Barkow and Regine Leibinger's design for a 1994 memorial to the Berlin Wall; a scheme which illustrates their understanding of the history and topography of this sensitive site as well as their American cultural training through their emphasis on landscape art.

Comprising a landscaped mound abutting a remaining segment of the Wall, it is more a monument than a building; an intervention on the largest scale, highlighting a phase of German history for later generations. The plateau, constructed of former East German prefab housing segments, smothers the site with a suitably ominous force, whilst occasional cuts and chasms criss-cross this historic site providing views. A wall of etched window panes bearing the names of all the Wall's victims proved too powerful for a jury that was more interested in a dignified memorial than an uncompromising political statement.

The shaping and marking of a landscape is also the subject of a small but challenging project for an entrance pavilion to the main Berlin Research Campus in the south-eastern suburb of Adlershof, where Wernher von Braun developed his rocket programme. All the buildings, dating back to the 1930s, are currently being restored and modernized and the pavilion is intended to capture visitors' attention. Its old function as a gatehouse, barring the institutes' entrance, is to be replaced by an open and welcoming sign, a ten metre high rectangular tower clad with frosted glass, whilst the single-storey pavilion will be refurbished and equipped with computer and communications technology.

What sets this and the previous project apart from their contemporaries' work are the remnants of obliterated history which Barkow and Leibinger locate and express through their designs; a skill more related to archaeology than architecture. The Bernauer Straße competition utilised the furrows in the mound to represent the major routes people took to cross the area before the Wall prevented them from doing so; whilst at Adlershof a secret tunnel is exposed, which was originally used to transport secret documents unnoticed across the busy road which bisects the research area. The design literally sheds light on the sites' past by positioning the glass tower directly above the entrance to this ominous underpass. Moreover, instead of hiding information from the general public the huge frosted panes of the tower will function as a display board advertising academic events and scientific facts. The tunnel, on the other hand, is scheduled to house an exhibition based on the institutes' illustrious past.

The unrelenting flatness of Berlin's sandy topography and its historically charged sites provokes a similar response from Barkow and Leibinger to that of the American landscape artists who were drawn to its deserts, investing the most uninhabitable places with simple but significant gestures.

ABOVE: Metal model; BELOW: Perspective (Bernauer Straße, Berlin); OPPOSITE, FROM ABOVE: Site plan; basement plan; cross section; INSETS, FROM ABOVE: Perspective from West; perspective from East (Adlershof Pavilion, Berlin)

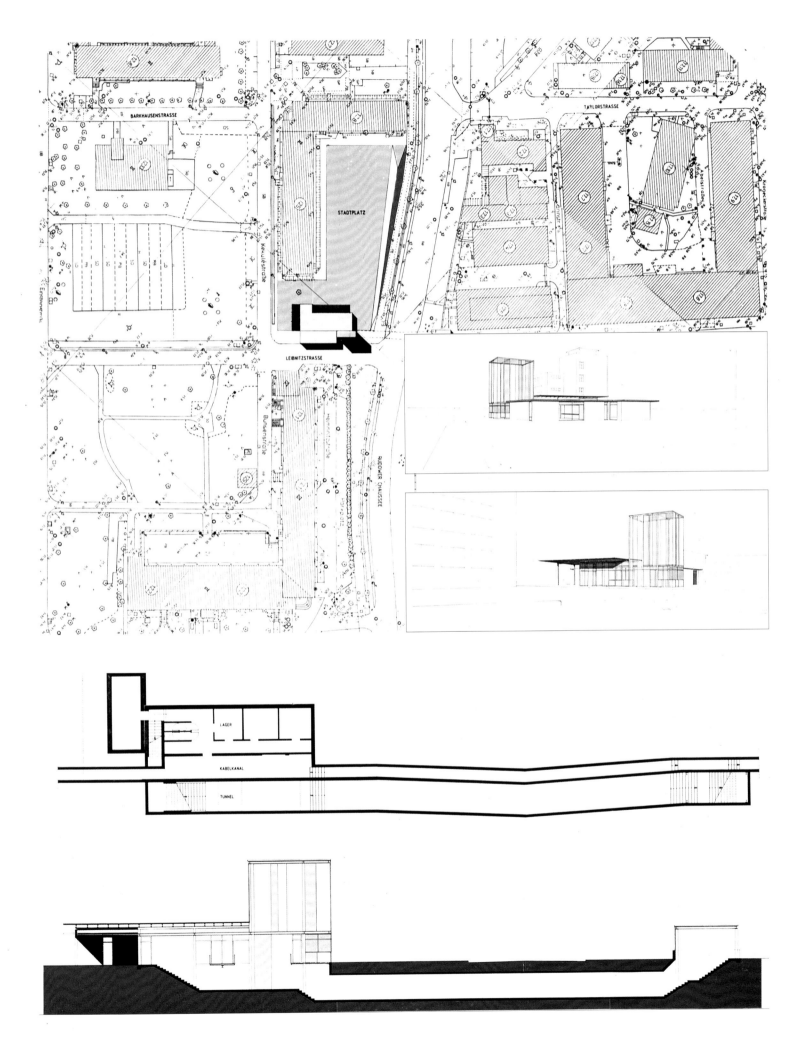

Huber and Staudt: Man and Machine

Throughout the 20th century, Berlin's attempts to establish a synthesis between nature and architecture has been increasingly threatened by the violent industrial exaltations of the Modernist Movement. This dichotomy has infiltrated the city's psyche to such an extent that it is still perceptible in contemporary Berlin.

However, with the emergence of the post-industrial society, the dialectic principle of man and machine has been replaced by the use of industrial metaphors in projects such as Christian Huber and Joachim Staudt's recent loft conversion. Constructed at the end of the last century, the original building was designed to take heavy industrial loads, utilising a heterogeneous structure comprised of cast-iron columns, a combined brick and steel frame-work and traditional brick vaulted ceilings. The contrast between this and the present inhabit-ant, a software company, could not be greater, yet this refurbishment is proof that architecture can assimilate such diversity. In fact, the designers have produced an extraordinary scheme within the constraints of a tight budget. For instance, the partitioning walls are all made of standard glazed elements alternating with dyed chipboard, arranged to incorporate standard doors and windows in each segment without overlapping.

A sense of order and an eye for structural division are also the prevailing design features in Huber and Staudt's Berlin research building. Here, despite the building's rigid design framework – based on a rectangular module derived from the structural frame – the layout incorporates two different functional zones separated by a generous circulation area; the first comprising laboratories and seminar rooms with a five metre ceiling and the other regular offices with a lower ceiling requirement of three metres. The building as a whole presents a strong and coherent bulwark against the urban piecemeal of the surrounding derelict harbour.

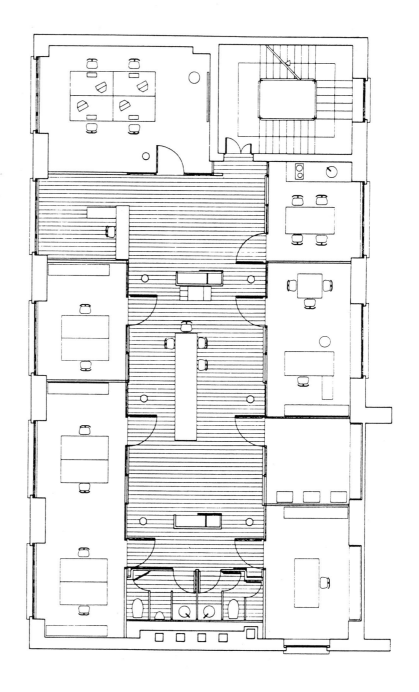

ABOVE: Floor plan; BELOW, FROM LEFT: Primary colour-coding; partitioning of old and new (loft conversion, Schinke Straße, Berlin); OPPOSITE: Model; model of typical floor (Research Institute, Berlin)

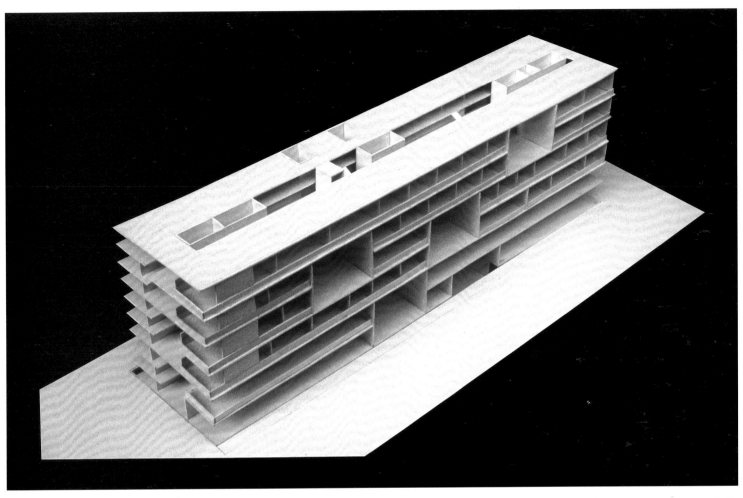

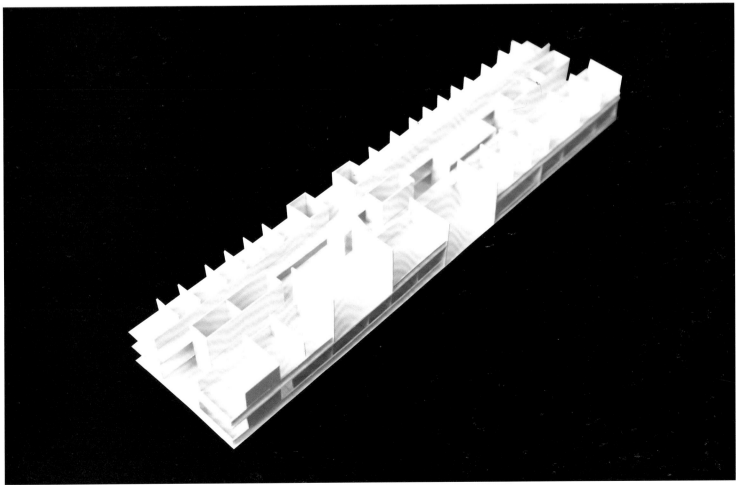

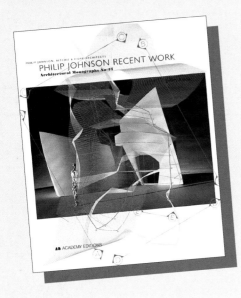

Soft Canopies

Detail in Building Series

Maritz Vandenberg

The second title in the *Detail in Building* series selects eight masterly examples of textile canopies from the contemporary work of leading international architects. Today the canopy remains a design detail of critical importance, yet one that is often designed to a lower standard than that of the building which it should enhance. As important today as in earlier centuries, the canopy in general is discussed in historical detail in the introductory essay, where examples provided by such masters as Alvar Aalto, Le Corbusier and Frank Lloyd Wright are analysed and set the context for the comparative studies. These include the Papal canopy, Bamberg, Germany by Frei Otto; the ticket office, Buckingham Palace, London by Michael Hopkins and Partners; and the Hajj Terminal, Saudi Arabia by SOM.

Detailed technical drawings are complemented by extensive photographic documentation in colour of built examples. The series will assist students and practitioners alike in resolving current design problems, providing a clear and comparative reference related to various structural solutions.

Maritz Vandenberg is an architect and author who has worked for *The Architect's Journal*.

Paperback 1 85490 440 X
245x245mm, 64 pages
Illustrated throughout
April 1996

What is Post-Modernism?

4th Edition

Charles Jencks

What is Post-Modernism? A question that has been asked with increasing frequency over the last 25 years now achieves a partial answer as it continues to evolve. In the fourth edition of his popular book, Charles Jencks, the main definer of Post-Modern architecture, considers the concept as it relates to the arts and literature and offers a spirited defence of the movement against the growing Modernist reaction. This completely revised text presents the reader with numerous new examples of art and architecture, as well as outlining the history which preceded it, facilitating a much clearer understanding of the overall concept.

Charles Jencks is well known as the author of the best-selling *The Language of Post-Modern Architecture* (6th Edition, 1991), *Architecture Today* (3rd Edition, 1994) and *The Architecture of the Jumping Universe* (1995), in addition to other highly acclaimed books on contemporary building and Post-Modern thought.

Paperback 1 85490 428 0
240x225mm, 68 pages
70 illustrations, mostly in colour
June 1996

Other titles in the *What Is?* series:

What is Abstraction?
What is Classicism?
What is Deconstruction?
What is Modernism?

Philip Johnson

Architectural Monograph No 44

Following a relatively late start in the world of architecture, Philip Johnson has since earned his reputation as the old master of modern architecture. It is widely accepted that he is more than just an architect, for he has combined the roles of architectural critic, historian, curator and patron. This volume concentrates on the latest manifestations in the work of this architectural chameleon. In an exclusive interview he reveals the methods of engineering and construction which have enabled him to realise his latest ideas and the thought processes which are already leading him to the next stage of his exciting career. Published to coincide with his 90th birthday, this monograph presents the work of a man always striving for new ideas with an energetic enthusiasm which is impressive and awesome.

Paperback 1 85490 284 9
305x252mm, 120 pages
Illustrated throughout, mostly in colour
June 1996

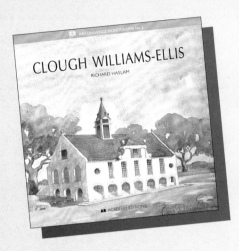

Erno Goldfinger
RIBA Drawings Monographs No 3

Robert Elwall

Clough Williams-Ellis
RIBA Drawings Monographs No 2

Richard Haslam

The second title in the RIBA Drawings Mono-graph series features the work of the Welsh architect, Clough Williams-Ellis. Widely known as the architect of Portmeirion, the Italianate holiday village in Wales featured in the TV series *The Prisoner*, he was a practising architect for 75 years and designed a wide range of buildings (houses, schools, churches, country houses), as well as gardens and gateways, furniture, lettering and monuments. Brought up in the country, he developed a great interest and concern for the environment and was a founder member of the Council for the Protection of Rural England and Rural Wales.

Richard Haslam has written on historic buildings – their architecture and restoration – in Wales, Italy and England and since 1984 has practised as a consultant in the use of build-ings by institutions. A major contributor to *Country Life* and author of a number of books on Welsh architecture and restoration, he was also a close neighbour of Clough Williams-Ellis for some years.

Paperback 1 85490 430 2
245x245mm, 112 pages
Over 80 illustrations, 38 in colour
April 1996

Born in Budapest, Erno Goldfinger studied architecture at the Ecole des Beaux-Arts in Paris in the 1920s at a time of great artistic ferment. Friendly with leading avant-garde figures such as Braque and Ozenfant, he helped to establish the breakaway atelier of Auguste Perret, the pioneer of reinforced concrete design, who was to be a major influence on his work. Schemes during this Parisian period include the remodelling of apartment interiors for fashionable clients such as Suzanne Blum, the lawyer confidante of the Duchess of Windsor, and the London salon of the beautician Helena Rubinstein. In 1934 he moved to London and unlike many other émigré architects who soon left, Goldfinger remained in practice here until his retirement in 1977. His career reveals a unique insight into the development of Modernism in the United Kingdom, illustrated in the beautiful collection of drawings and sketches held by the British Architectural Library at the Royal Institute of British Architects, in London.

Robert Elwall is the Photographs Curator at the British Architectural Library, and has curated and written the accompanying catalogues for numerous architectural exhibitions including *Unlocking the Thirties* (1979) and *Pavilions Near and Far* (1992).

Paperback 1 85490 444 2
245x245mm, 112 pages
Over 80 illustrations, 38 in colour
April 1996

Previously published in the RIBA Drawings Monographs series:
Sketches by Edwin Lutyens
Margaret Richardson

To be published later in 1996:
Christopher Nicholson
Neil Bingham

Further information can be obtained from Academy Group Ltd, 42 Leinster Gardens, London W2 3AN, Tel: 0171 402 2141 Fax: 0171 723 9540, or from your local sales office:

National Book Network Inc, 4720 Boston Way, Lanham, Maryland 20706, Tel: (301) 459 3366 Fax: (301) 459 2118;

VCH, Boschstrasse 12, Postfach 101161, 69451 Weinheim, Federal Republic of Germany, Tel: +49 6201 606 144 Fax: +49 6201 606 184;

THE LIMIT; Engineering on the Boundaries of Science, Mike Dash, BBC Publications, 191pp, b/w and col ills, HB, £17.99

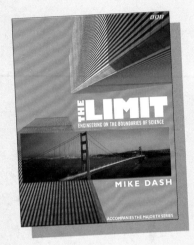

Like art, until recently, architecture was seldom treated seriously as a subject for mass consumption. Art hit the headlines when it was stolen, when a 'ridiculously high price' was paid for it or when it crossed the boundaries of 'morality'. Architecture reached the tabloids for different reasons. It could not be 'stolen' etc, but because it is 'public art' there was more opportunity for 'Outraged, from Wilsden'-type critiques. 'Outraged' has become more eloquent through 'consumer's voice' magazines such as *Which* and the manifestation of this change has brought architecture into our sitting rooms.

The viewing figures for the BBC2 series on engineers *The Limit* were, as the programme board had presumably anticipated when they chose the 'prime time' eight pm Tuesday slot, extraordinarily high. Engineers and architects were presented as exciting futurists rather than as the spotty scientists and dreary draughtsmen of old. Narrated by Robbie Coltrane, *The Limit* was sensationalist only in that it focused on the extremes: the tallest building; the largest aeroplane; the trickiest tunnel; the longest bridge; remotest robot and the fastest ship. Even the elevator music that accompanied some of the shots hardly detracts from the contagious sense of excitement in Coltrane's voice as he said: 'Obayashi engineers of Japan and Norman Foster have combined to design a tower that will contain a town the size of Guilford. But how can they avoid the people on the top floors being thrown about in the wind, and how can it survive the earthquakes that are threatening Japan?'

The engineer Kazo Shimizu, whose charisma was 'better' for television than Foster's more measured stance, was portrayed as an affable *Back to the Future* type scientist, willing to be a guinea pig for progress as he 're-lived' Japan's most recent earthquake in a simulator. But his conclusion that the higher a building the more the effects of the earthquake will be dampened – because although the ground vibrations are very rapid, the top of the Millennium Tower takes six to eight seconds to move from side to side – revealed a logical mind, unhampered by conventional beliefs. The question of earthquakes was answered at the end where we learned that discussions with North American client are underway to relocate Millennium Tower to China. However, this uncertainty is an endemic problem with such challenges. Will the world's largest aircraft ever be built if it requires its airport destinations to make major adaptations to accommodate it? Will funds be made available for a small drill to land on comet Wirtanen as it travels a 100 times faster than a speeding bullet? Will anyone want to live a kilometre high?

Mike Dash, is the author of the accompanying book. I say accompanying, but because of the above mentioned uncertainties and nature of publishing, the book was actually completed before the series was finalised – a chicken and egg situation. Unlike most television-tie in material therefore, Dash's writing is lateral in the extreme. His approach to the Millennium Tower starts with the French daredevil tightrope walker, Philippe Petit who 'breathed deeply and stepped off the parapet into space' as he walked between the twin towers of the 150-storey World Trade Centre in New York. Dash communicates a more tangible sense of height in words than all the weird and wonderful camera angles could on the screen. But television is new to the subject. Books have been written about architecture since the wigwam, but *The Limit* is only the tip of the television iceberg and the potential symbiosis between these everyday forms of art is enormous. The Millennium Tower is an extreme example but other developments in architecture could easily sustain thorough and stimulating television treatment. Let's hope that the success of *The Limit* will encourage television companies to invest in this neglected subject, consummate with the evolving public interests of the 90s.
K MacInnes

THE SPACE OF APPEARANCE, George Baird, MIT Press, 400pp, 149 b/w ills, HB, £38.50

This is a difficult book, part beginner's guide and part academic treatise. A dense theoretical ramble introduces what could be a series of enjoyable chapters on facets of architecture, from private to public.

Out with post-structuralists such as Jacques Derrida and Jean Baudrillard and their nihilistic detachment, Professor Baird argues in his introduction. In instead, with the ideas of Hannah Arendt as a philosophical divining light, a touchstone of architectural interpretation and development.

Relatively obscure today, Arendt was well-known in the 50s and 60s as a thinker who broadened the inward-looking existentialism of the likes of Jean Paul Sartre into a social theory of self-discovery. A German who fled the Nazis in 1941, she first made her name studying the social decay that led to totalitarianism. In perhaps her seminal work *The Human Condition* (1958) she argued that people defined themselves not by introspection but through social interaction.

The title *The Space of Appearance* is drawn from Arendt's work, which Baird extrapolates to encompass architecture. Put simply, buildings are an inevitable determinant of how people interact in the public realm and should be conceived and interpreted as such. If only it were put simply. Baird's style is hugely off-putting; familiarity with abstruse academic concepts is taken as read, whilst the text is pretentious and immensely confusing.

After all this, the first chapter 'Life as a Work of Art' comes as something of a relief. From here, the book is essentially a collection of essays on various architectural ideas from the last couple of hundred years. From Jeremy Bentham's panoptic prisons to Venturi's promotion of pop-culture, Baird shows how ideas about the nature of society have been made manifest in bricks, mortar and chain link fencing.

The book's structure works well. Starting with the private house – the bourgeois villas of Olbrich and Le Corbusier – it progresses, via institutional buildings like the Pompidou Centre and the Casa del Fascista, to the public arena of the modern city shopping centre. Some chapters are straight historical narratives given a critical twist, whereas others – the chapter on architecture and politics, for instance – cover broader ground.

For me, the best chapter is the discussion of organic architecture, the anti-urban, back-to-nature ideas exemplified by the later work of Frank Lloyd Wright. Illustrating that Broadacre City, Wright's chilling Utopia, represents contemporary car-driven suburban life. This is the one chapter that told me something new, but generally Baird's analysis in hardly original.

With refinement, the essays might make for an introductory course for students on the relationship between architecture, culture and society. Indeed, given Baird's Harvard professorship, the book probably originated as a lecture series.

But as it stands, despite the excellent illustrations throughout, the book is repetitive and contains overly long chunks of quotation and academic jargon which often conspires to make interesting ideas quite tedious.
V Perry

DESIGNING MODERNITY; The Arts of Reform and Persuasion 1885-1945, Ed Wendy Kaplan, Thames and Hudson, 352pp, 417 ills (300 colour) HB, £38.00

Designing Modernity attempts to, and largely succeeds in, condensing the complex relationship between politics, social control and the aesthetics of art and design between 1885 and 1945. The book's inspiration and material is selected directly from the Wolfsonian Institute in Miami; a unique collection of objects dedicated to examining the socio-political implications of design in this period.

Written information is presented in a collection of essays by leading social and art historians (for example, Dennis P Doordan's 'Political Things: Design in Fascist Italy' and John Heskett's 'Design in Inter-War Germany') within three significant sections: 'Confronting Modernity', 'Celebrating Modernity' and 'Manipulating Modernity: Political Persuasion'. Through the appraisal of the wide variety products and graphic design, the advance of modern, materially-oriented civilisation is plotted, with particular attention paid to the impact of such progress on the masses at large and the ways in which the powers that be employed new aesthetic trends to further their ideological aspirations.

Finding the right balance between sufficient historico-political detail – which is exhaustively stimulating in light of two World Wars and the rise of Fascism – and generating sufficient interest in the products

themselves sometimes leaves the reader a little dissatisfied on both counts. However, extensive essay notes and a 'checklist' of exhibition objects provide ample opportunity for further study, while generous illustrations provide the necessary visual stimulation.
L Ryan

HISTORY AS HOT NEWS; The World of the Early Victorians Through the Eyes of the Illustrated London News, 1842-1865, Leonard de Vries, John Murray Publishers, 160pp, b/w ills, PB, £14.99

This book gives us a remarkably vivid picture of how people, for the first time, received in visual form news of both dramatic and everyday events from home and abroad. A brief foreword by Arthur Bryant followed by a substantial contents list is all that precede the news stories and images taken straight from *The Illustrated London News*.

The news is still as exciting today as it would have been the day it was printed: the attempted assassination of Queen Victoria; the 1848 revolution in Paris; the Crimean War; inventions of all kinds including the elevator and the ascent of Monsieur Poiteven on horseback in a balloon.

The Illustrated London News constitutes what is probably the most important pictorial source for the social history of any age or country. Although the illustrations are captivating, it is the journalism, which was subjected to the opinions and speculation of the writer, that holds the element of excitement. The variety of 'reporters' for *The Illustrated London News* did not adhere to a journalistic integrity that we take for granted in today's newspapers and publications. The reports were biased and sensationalist, politics were suspect and the gore was bloody.
C Fontoura

100 MASTERPIECES; FURNITURE THAT MADE THE 20TH CENTURY
Design Museum, April-September 1996

Most designers are aware that there is a symbiotic relationship between buildings and furniture, epitomised by those architects who have conceived their buildings and furniture as a homogenous whole; Charles Rennie Mackintosh's Argyle Street Tea Rooms, Glasgow, 1911, or Richard Roger's Lloyd's Building, 1986, for instance. Extreme examples admittedly but there are numerous architects who have turned their hand to designing furniture, ranging from Aalto to Venturi, Wright to Gehry. Similarly there have been many furniture designers who have designed buildings, which provide the perfect backdrop for their own creations; Philippe Starck being one of the most notable protagonists, whose extravagant and dramatic architecture – such as *Le Baron Vert*, Osaka 1990, and *La Flamme*, Tokyo 1989 – continues to challenge and amaze. Although all of the above have been well documented, until now there have been few exhibitions which have systematically explored this relationship in any detail.

Featuring celebrated examples chosen from the unrivalled collection of the Vitra Design Museum, Germany, and designed by Richard Greenwood, '100 Masterpieces' examines the development of furniture from 1850 to the present day, focusing in particular on the influence of technological developments on design, and includes designs by Le Corbusier, Charles and Ray Eames, Marcel Breuer and Coop Himmelblau. '100 Masterpieces' is of interest to both designers and architects as it provides the perfect opportunity to examine these rare pieces of furniture; seeing them in three dimensions rather than two. Highlighting the relationship between architecture and furniture, this exhibition should bring a fresh perspective to both disciplines, promoting innovative and invigorating designs.

 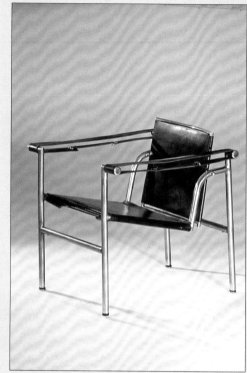

FROM ABOVE, LEFT TO RIGHT: Jean Prouve, 1928; Le Corbusier/Charlotte Perriand/Pierre Jeanneret, Fauteuil a Dossier Basculant, 1928; Marcel Breuer, Chaise No 313, 1932; Alvar Aalto, Chaise No 39, 1936

GAMES OF ARCHITECTURE

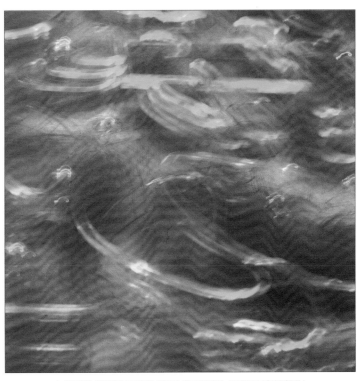

A. TOPOS, INFORMATION FIELD, NATIONAL MUSEUM OF KOREA

Architectural Design

GAMES OF ARCHITECTURE

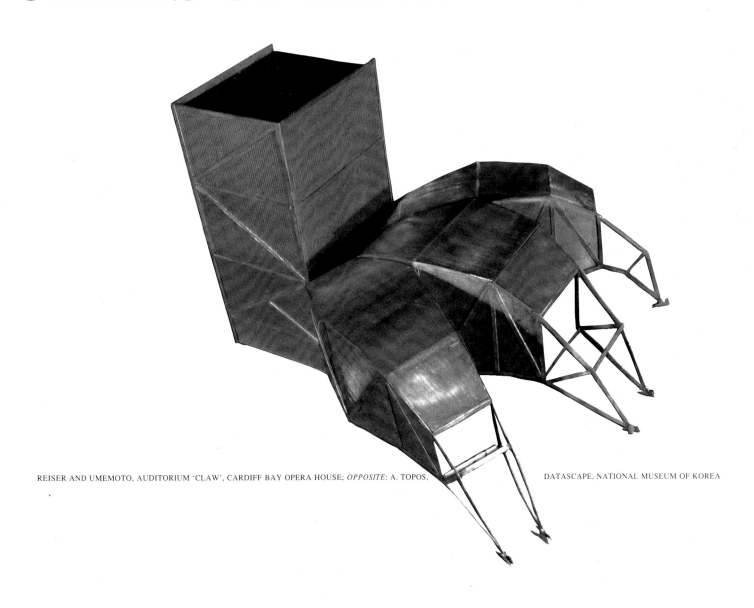

REISER AND UMEMOTO, AUDITORIUM 'CLAW', CARDIFF BAY OPERA HOUSE; *OPPOSITE*: A. TOPOS, DATASCAPE, NATIONAL MUSEUM OF KOREA

ACADEMY EDITIONS • LONDON

Acknowledgements

We would like to thank Jane Harrison and David Turnbull for their enthusiasm in producing this issue and all the contributors involved. All material is courtesy of the authors and architects unless otherwise stated.

The guest-producers would particularly like to thank: Madeline Gins and Armand Schwerner for their support and encouragement; Alastair Brotchie of Atlas Press for his generous assistance in contacting members of the Ou.Li.Po., Ou.Pein.Po. and Ou.Pho.Po. groups in Paris, for the wealth of material contained within the Atlas publications which he made available to them and for providing the material for 'Seine'; Evans and Wong, Paris, for assistance in obtaining the images for 'Come Clean'; Deborah Treisman of *Grand Street* for her kind help in contacting and obtaining various permissions, in particular for the Virilio/Sans interview; the Virginia Zabrieski Gallery, New York, for assistance in contacting Joan Fontcuberta, and Diverse Works in Houston for providing the material on Project Row Houses.

'Algorithms of Beauty' image *p9* appears courtesy of Heidi Gilpin/William Forsythe of the Frankfurt Ballet. 'Architecture' is extracted from Daniel Spoerri in collaboration with Robert Filliou, Emmett Williams and Dieter Roth, *An Anecdoted Topography of Chance*, Atlas Press, 1996, reproduced with the publisher's permission. 'City' *p17*, 'Klapper Hall' *p45* and 'Storefront' *p92* images appear courtesy of Barbara Gladstone Gallery, New York. 'Games of Love and Chance' is extracted from *Grand Street*, Grand Street Press, (New York) Spring 1995 reproduced with permission from Virilio and Sans. 'Goose Game' images *pp36-38* appear courtesy of Claire Robinson. 'Negotiation' is extracted from Rem Koolhaas and Bruce Mau, *S, M, L, XL*, Monacelli Press inc, (New York) 1995 reproduced with permission of Rem Koolhaas. 'Remainder, The' is extracted from Jean-Jacques Lecercle, *The Violence of Language*, Routledge, (London) 1990, reproduced with his permission.

Photographic Credits: All material is courtesy of the authors and architects unless otherwise stated.
P Warchol *p11* 'Angst Cartography', *p56* 'Monumental Propaganda', *p66* 'Penny Screen'; S Muto *p15* 'Bottles', *p17* 'Chaos', *pp53-55* 'Micro-Macro'; Matt Wargo *p16* 'Bricks'; Sue Barr *p22* 'Flatscape', *pp60-61* 'Negotiation'; Joshua White *pp47, 50* 'Lewis House'.

Front Cover: a. topos, (Com)pression zones and pressure points, National Museum of Korea

EDITOR: Maggie Toy
EDITORIAL TEAM: Stephen Watt, Ramona Khambatta
ART EDITOR: Andrea Bettella CHIEF DESIGNER: Mario Bettella DESIGNER: Gregory Mills

CONSULTANTS: Catherine Cooke, Terry Farrell, Kenneth Frampton, Charles Jencks, Heinrich Klotz, Leon Krier, Robert Maxwell, Demetri Porphyrios, Kenneth Powell, Colin Rowe, Derek Walker

First published in Great Britain in 1996 by *Architectural Design* an imprint of
ACADEMY GROUP LTD, 42 LEINSTER GARDENS, LONDON W2 3AN
Member of the VCH Publishing Group
ISBN: 1 85490 255 5 (UK)

Copyright © 1996 Academy Group Ltd. *All rights reserved*
The entire contents of this publication are copyright and cannot be reproduced
in any manner whatsoever without written permission from the publishers

The Publishers and Editor do not hold themselves responsible for the opinions expressed by the writers of articles or letters in this magazine
Copyright of articles and illustrations may belong to individual writers or artists
Architectural Design Profile 121 is published as part of *Architectural Design* Vol 66 5-6/1996
Architectural Design Magazine is published six times a year and is available by subscription

Distributed to the trade in the United States of America by
NATIONAL BOOK NETWORK INC, 4720 BOSTON WAY, LANHAM, MARYLAND, 20706

Printed and bound in Italy

Contents

ARCHITECTURAL DESIGN PROFILE No 121

GAMES OF ARCHITECTURE

Guest-Producers
Jane Harrison/David Turnbull

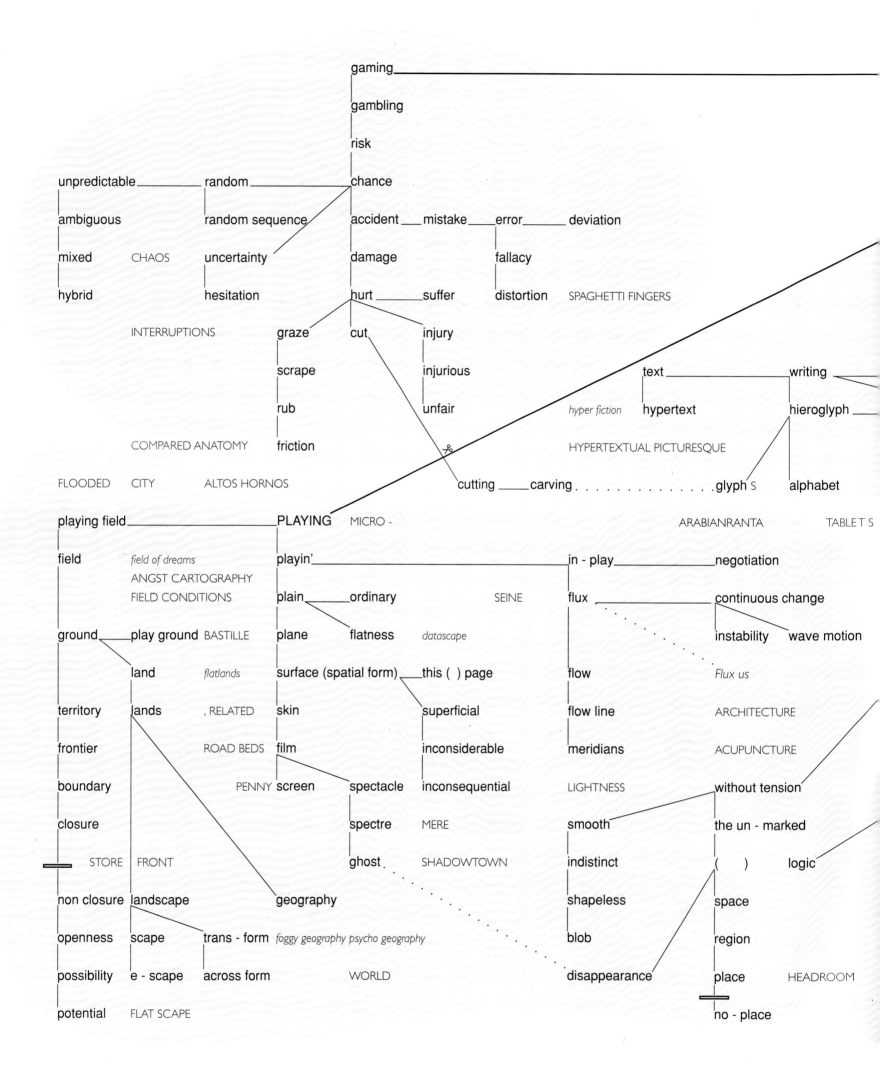

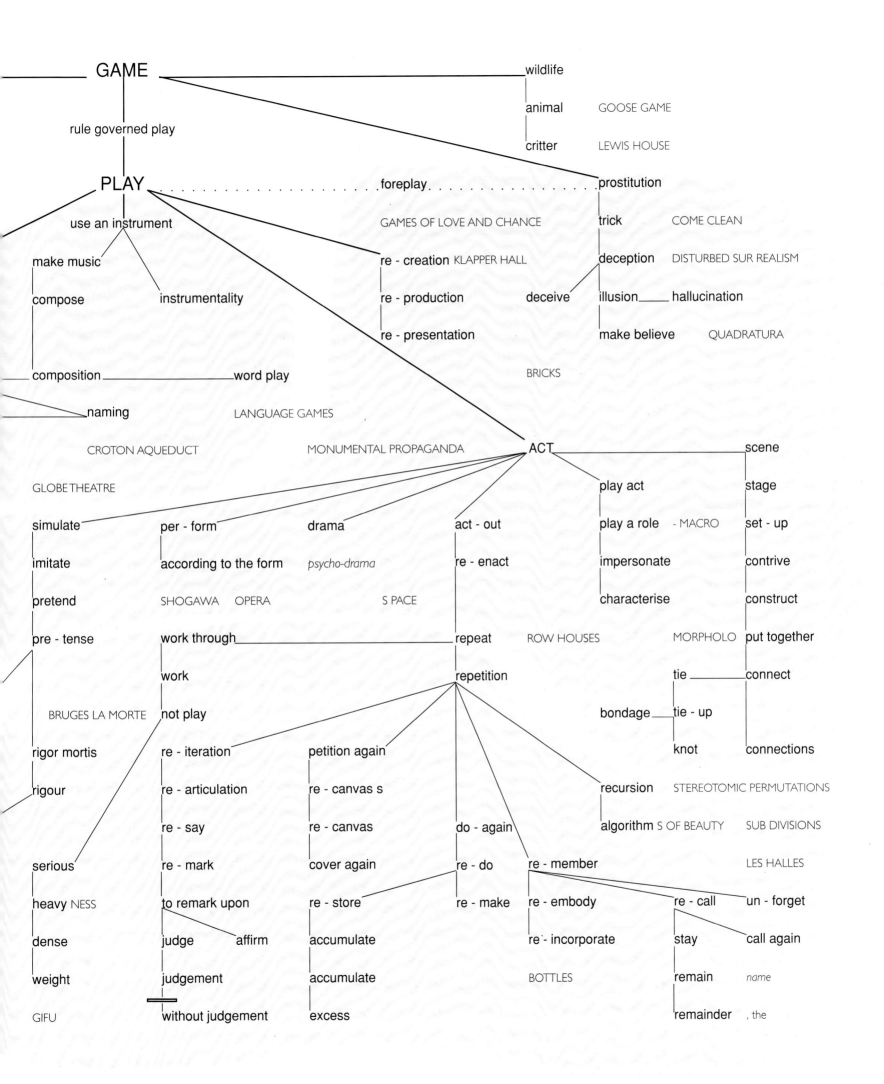

AS . . .

Jane Harrison/David Turnbull

Paul Virilio states in *The Art of the Motor* (University of Minnesota Press, 1995 p141): 'In Merleau-Ponty's phenomenology of perception, we find the idea Husserl shared that space is limited to the world of sensory experience and that beyond this there is no space worthy of the name, only the excess of a "time depth": universal time, which has nothing in common with the void of so-called cosmic space. But today, with INFORMATION as the last dimension of space-time-matter, it is very tempting for infonauts to identify this spaceless time depth with information that is no longer restricted but has become generalised'.

Not space as emptiness, rather space as fullness. The boundaries between different realities have become blurred and it has become increasingly difficult to distinguish between what is merely information and what is concrete; between reality and some temporary alternate reality, hallucination or dream. It is clear that new, optimistic ways of dealing with excess must be found, to determine new potentialities. There must not be a retreat from the issue into the reassurance of exclusion, restriction and reduction, but rather the possibilities for pleasure and the freedom to perpetually reconstruct reality, mining the depthless space of information which should be opened up. This issue of *Architectural Design* addresses this task. It is a sampler, an interconnected but digressive web of material drawn from an extended field, including architecture. The focus, regardless of the source of the material, is emphatically on the potential for architecture.

In the centre lies the emergence of what Jerome Sans in conversation with Paul Virilio, **Games of Love and Chance** (pp24-26) calls a fully fledged aesthetics of play. This is both explored and challenged in the course of the conversation. Virilio's working definition of play lies somehow beyond pleasure, in the play of a machine component loose in its housing – a metaphor for an unprecedented mobility in relation to reality. Jennifer Bloomer develops connections between the garden, the game and the space of information, a co-mingling of old and new, the seamlessness of time and space, **The Hypertextual Picturesque** (pp43-44). The persistence of the old is seen here in relation to the subtly new issue of play. If thinking about the garden serves as a link to the vastness, the proliferation and mutation of electronic space, play in all its incredible variety, and at its most extreme, is sponsored by the city. This is where Sanford Kwinter begins in **Play Time** (pp65-66). Like Christian Hubert in **Playtime** (p66), Kwinter discusses play in relation to Winnicott's distinction between a thing found in the world and something made up; a distinction that must have been, in a sense, already universally abandoned. The fullness of space beyond bodily experience, beyond what is known of the world, is represented in outsider art. The outsider's delirious involvement in the super abundance of possible experiences as well as actual experience, where what is made up is simultaneously understood to have been found in the world, forms the basis of Christine Wertheim's paper, **S pace** (pp78-83).

Field Conditions (p21) defines field configurations as 'loosely bounded aggregates characterised by porosity and local connectivity'. The field, the glyph and the tablet have become the keywords for us, where field + glyph = tablet. The glyph is understood here, as an extreme condensation of (dream) thoughts. **Globe Theatre** (p35) and **Tablets** (p94) exemplify the expansive surface with local depths (knots) that this equation implies, materialising and giving weight to varying intensities of connection; connections which simultaneously separate (see **Language-Games**, p46), making space at the site of maximum compression. A word web (pp6-7) structures possible interconnections between the contributions which have been arranged in alphabetical order around the essays. A definition of **Architecture** (p15), **Come Clean** (pp18-19) and **The Remainder** (pp72-73), by Jean-Jacques Lecercle) serve as reminders or questions and are the gateways, entry points into the web. They also emphasise a persistent theme,

that the **Mere** . . . (p53) is not mere. The forgotten, the undervalued or the suppressed will surface in the course of the Game. Keywords at the bottom of each contribution relate back to the word web and suggest linkages. There is no planned sequence for reading but there are many signposts. Like the non-places described by anthropologist Marc Auge, this atypical zone is defined by its instructions for use. This introductory text is extended to re-appear at intervals, which are marked A 1-4, **Flatscape** (p22), **Glyphs** (p35), **Table** t (p93) and **World:** (p94).

Flatscapes and **Road Bed S** (p74-75) are alphabets, infrastructures of the infra-ordinary. **Headroom** (p38) is an accumulation. Some contributions point, indicating potential, some are strategies for producing effects, some are the results of these strategies, some are combinations: Urban **Acupuncture** (p9) points, like hot spots in an architectural hyper-fiction, local interventions make their greatest impact elsewhere. The make believe meridians of the city are the conduits for the distribution of effect. **Related Lands** (p71) is a reconfiguring of the globe as the intersection of both mental and real maps. The explicit, excessive use of games in the work of the Frankfurt Ballet allows a work to unfold as the author/choreographer disappears. **Algorithms of Beauty** (p9) is a brief introduction to this, discussed in relation to the Game of Life. The game in this instance is also a psychological safety net, making it possible to lose control without losing control. **Flooded City** (p23) starts with an algorithm – put something in water and see what happens. In *Ulysses*, by James Joyce (the uncorrected text, first published 1922, Paladin, 1992, p782), 'What did Bloom do at the range?' . . . water flowed to connect every thing to everything else. A map of place names along the **Croton Aqueduct** (p20) part of the New York water system, which suggests new programmes and new social spaces associated with this piece of infrastructure, acknowledges a 'foggy geography', the uncanny persistence of meaning in place names described by Michel de Certeau in *The Practice of Everyday Life* (Berkeley, University of California Press, 1984, pp104-5): 'a strange toponymy that is detached from actual places and flies high over the city'.

Jennifer Bloomer has written elsewhere (*Architecture and the Text: The (S)crypts of Joyce and Piranesi*, Yale University Press, 1993, p82) about the site of the games(s) as 'The Gate to the Underworld' – the game as an opening to the unconscious. Photographs in the series **Altos Hornos** (p10) manipulate material from the setting to be photographed itself, directly on the photographic surface. These images are not so much of the city as from it, an accumulation of accurate impressions. **Compared Anatomy** (p20) gives a terrifying indication of their potential force. The recognition of animal forms in the flowing surfaces of the **Lewis House** (pp47-50) is as disturbing as the potential implications of anamorphosis in **Stereotomic Permutations** (pp89-91). **Subdivisions** (p93) explores the psychological effects of suburban housing arrangements.

The renewed interest in the fantastic writings of Calvino and Borges, the alternate realities of Philip K Dick or J G Ballard, and the popularity of science fiction, which parallels official discussion of Cyberspace, is clearly a manifestation of the collapse of the distinction between the made up and the found in the world. **Angst Cartography** (pp10-11) intersects a fantastic text (by Calvino) with material drawn from the abandoned Gowanus Canal in New York constructing a 'field of dreams' – a dreamscape which is nevertheless explicitly concerned with the physical setting itself. **Monumental Propaganda** (p56) and **Penny Screen** (p64) reuse the thrown away, the overturned ideology or the valueless coin as their material. The disregarded artefact performs as a 'glyph', a concentration of thoughts.

As it is played out in the real world with real players, the Game has clear political implications, acknowledging excess and complication as facts of architectural practice, not fictions . . .

(continued on page 95)

ACUPUNCTURE, URBAN

James Williamson

An attempt to map onto the city another urban structure of association and recall based upon the banal and everyday; the un-
eventful, the personal and the intimate rather than the public. It
proposes a reminder of what may constitute the real life of the
city, the multiple, unseen connections within the tissue of its existence: 49 unclaimed bodies in a Chicago heat wave, a random
act of decency, a beloved pet . . . These are marked by a structured index: shadow (a bank president's office on a parking deck),
event (4th December the conception of daughter, Jenny), objects
(locks of hair, a packet of cigarettes, a tattered paperback novel
of no particular interest) and marks (a line between the place
Jenny was born and the place she was last seen). Interventions in
the city that might have a more profound and measurable impact
elsewhere, other than the site of the intervention . . . travelling
along what might be seen as the meridians of the city to transfer
their effects.

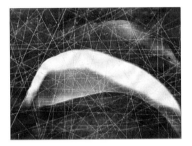

Key words : connections . flow line . meridians

ALGORITHMS OF BEAUTY

Heidi Gilpin

a   Logical arithmetical or computational procedure that if cor-
    rectly applied ensures the solution of a problem.
b   Recursive procedure whereby an infinite sequence of terms
    can be generated.
ex Take an equation, solve it, take the result and fold it back into
    the equation and then solve it again. Keep doing this a mil-
    lion times and see what happens.

The use of games, and in particular the use of rules – an excess
of as well as a sanctioned breaking of – are central to the recent
compositional and architectural strategies employed by William
Forsythe and the Frankfurt Ballet. In the context of this work,
games are used as architectural, mnemonic, political, visual and
dynamic devices in the process of developing movement and
material during both the preparation and the performance of a
production. Such strategies of gaming confuse issues of authority and autonomy in the process of composition.

  The Frankfurt Ballet's production *Eidos:Telos*, 1995, involves
complex systems of organisation, intricate models of material
and associative structures and a highly developed form of agency
on the part of each dancer, who interact with, and produce,
material based on the algorithmic systems of construction created for the production. The performance of these systems en-
acts a dynamic visual picture similar to Conway's 'Game of Life',
a computer game based on algorithmic function. In *Eidos:Telos* a
kind of default-consciousness evolves in the participants, whereby
the decision making process is woven into the compositional
system in a way that enables alternatives to develop simultaneously to the defined possibilities. This production is derived from
material within these formational systems from video, film, my-
thology, critical theory and philosophy, mathematics, literature,
architectural forms and deformations and computer-based
interactivity visible only to the dancers during the performance,
as well as sonic, visual and spatial triggers whose formulations
are based on constructed systems of composition.

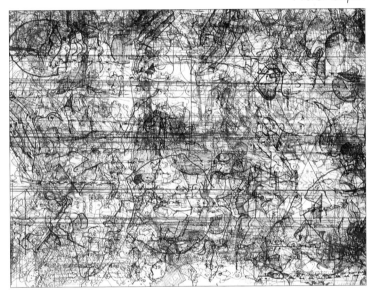

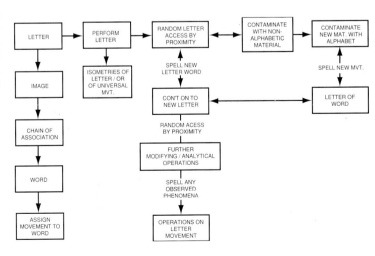

Key words : algorithm . excess . playing field . repetition

9

ALTOS HORNOS, BILBAO

Joan Fontcuberta

 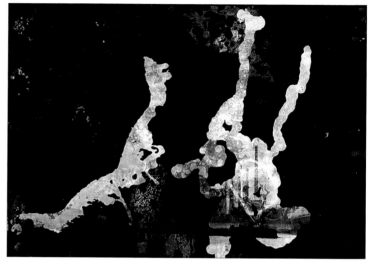

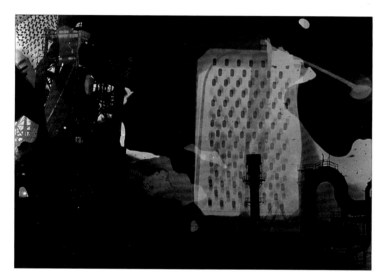 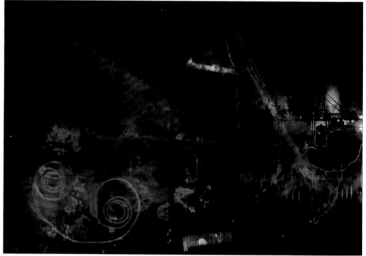

Key words : city . damage . friction

ANGST CARTOGRAPHY, FIELD OF DREAMS

Baratloo and Balch

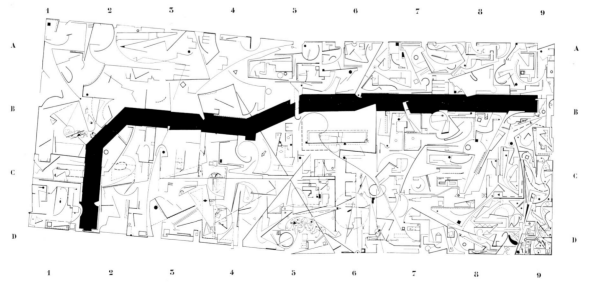

ANGST CARTOGRAPHY

Baratloo and Balch

> One late afternoon in August of 1982,
>
> A2   D8   B1   A1   D9   B4   C7   B7   C4
>
> while walking among the post-industrial
>
> A8   C5   A6   D5   C9   D2   A4   B8   C1
>
> ruins of the Gowanus Canal area in Brooklyn,
>
> A5   B5   D4   D1   D7   A3   C8   C2   A7
>
> we realized that we had come upon
>
> B9   B6   B3   C3   D6   C6   D3   B2   A9
>
> one of Italo Calvino's <u>Invisible Cities</u>.

This 11 year project started in 1982 with a contribution for the exhibition 'The Monument Redefined' which involved a visionary cartographic projection, or 'Big Map' (91x152cm), juxtaposed with images of the Gowanus Canal section of Brooklyn – with its abandoned industrial heritage and maze-like streets – and Italo Calvino's story *Cities & Desire 5*. In 1988, moving off-site for an installation at the PS1 Museum, the Big Map was divided into 36 quadrants, encased in welded steel and located within the building's labyrinthine stairs and hallways; transforming the museum into a metaphorical site between Calvino's fiction, the Gowanus Canal and its representation in *ANGST Cartography*. The installation underwent its third major conceptualization in 1989, this time into book form, issued by SITES Books. For publication, Baratloo and Balch printed negative images of the canal and its surrounding industrial structures and paired them with the cartographic plates. Calvino's story was separated into 36 single-line segments, breaking the text's conventional format, which was then applied as sub-text and titles.

ANGST: Cartography (Field of Dreams) a mobile installation first shown at Princeton University's School of Architecture, 1992, utilizes a system of clamps, frames and collapsible podiums to display each of the 36 field components – photo, map and text. These are arranged in a random sequence to abstractly re-configure the site, exploiting the characteristics of the exhibition space as well as its relationship to the system of circulation and closure: visitors explore the gallery through the resultant maze, whilst they conceptually navigate *ANGST* itself.

Key words : chance . field . writing

ARABIANRANTA, HELSINKI

Chora/Raoul Bunschoten

Helsinki is confronting many new forces including ecological issues, urban icon formation and city management, large-scale economic developments and geo-political changes. These imperatives compel the city to test out new strategic planning proposals that can deal with such issues whilst acting as an example to other cities in the European Community or Russia. It is with these in mind that Chora developed a strategic planning model of negotiation for Helsinki.

RIGHT: Scenario (i) – Bird migration

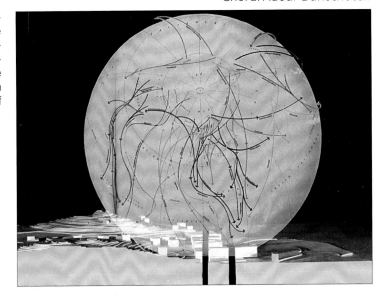

ARABIANRANTA

A Movement of Helsinki
Helsinki was founded here in the year 1550 but was later settled further south on the peninsula.

B Creation of new land
Dumping of the Arabia Factory waste as landfill has constantly moved the bay shoreline eastwards.

C Seasonal bird migration
Vanhankaupunginlahti bird reserve is 'an important resting area for migratory birds.'

D City plan for Viikki
The controversial proposal to create a new township of 13,000 residents and 6,000 workplaces in the vicinity of the bird reserve has resulted in a juridical complaint to EU.

E Increasing pressure for recreation

F Electronic tracking of birds
So called 'satellite birds' carry a small radio sender and can be traced all around the world by satellites.

G Strengthening of preservation
The bird reserve has been listed in international RAMSAR agreement for wetlands.

H Nesting of 60 bird species
'The area contains an unusual mix of species from the outer archipelago and agricultural environment.'

I Arctic research
'We are not that far from the idea of the area (high tech), we'd like to be a part of the plan.' Interview with Anders Backlund, Project Engineer, Kvaerner Masa Yards Inc.

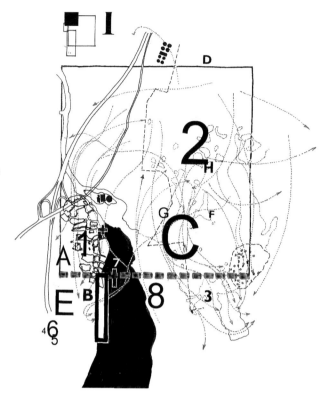

1 Old City Historic Area
Weaving factory
Old Church foundations
Mill
Museum of technology

2 Bird Reserve
'The most important single nature conservation area is the Viikin-Vanhankaupunginlahden area which is listed under the International Ramsar agreement as being an area of major importance for waterfowl.'
Helsinki Urban Guide, Helsinki City Planning Office, 1994

3 Ornithological Society/Suomen Birdlife

4 City Environment Office

5 City Planning Office

6 EU Directive: Bird Environments/World Wildlife Fund
Factor recently (1995) having jurisdiction in Finland.

7 Kvaerner Masa Yard/Arctic Research Institute
A specialised institute with efficient facilities and 16 employees, started in 1983.

8 Individual Recreational Users
The area is important for the neighbourhood and for the whole eastern part of the inner city.

A Official city plans
The Arabianranta plan has been accepted by the City Planning Board and is waiting acceptance by the City Parliament. The Herttoniemenranta plan is being realised.

B Community plan
20.9.1995: a meeting and workshop in the Into-gallery (UIAH) was organised by Toukola-seura, aiming to create an alternative plan.

C Proposed relocation of the harbour
'There are plans to transfer Helsinki's harbour activities to Vuosaari.'
Helsinki City Guide

D Extending recycling
In the premises of former Kyläsaari waste burning plant a recycling centre is working. A linear area for small recycling companies is being set up next to the centre.

E Pollution
'The clay coming from Vantaanjoki makes Vanhankaupginlahti relatively grey but it is slowly getting cleaner. Also the bird fauna using water plants is recovering.'
Matti Mieminen

F Landscape (horizon)

G Public space
20.9.1995: the fact that a community meeting took place in UIAH's Into-gallery reflects the need for public space in the Toukola area.

H UIAH/Gateway II Conference
' . . . cities are going through dramatic economic and cultural change that demand completely new ways of management . . . '
Gateway II, Managing Urban Change brochure, Sept 14-15, 1995

I Formulation of new planning body and urban icon

1 Arabia/UIAH
Model Condition: negotiated spatial and institutional relationship between Arabia and UIAH.

2 Open land
The landscape of the bay and bird reserve continues to the fields of Viikki.

3 Herttoniemi suburb
A 50s suburb with an ageing population of 8,000. A large extension is under construction.

4 Kivinokka
Small summer cottages which can be rented on trade union land.

5 Kulosaari
'The' upper class housing area in Helsinki. It was founded as an individual garden city municipality.

6 Leposaari Cemetery
The Island of the Dead in front of Kulosaari.

7 Metro

8 Zoo

9 Lulosaari Bridge

10 Hanasaari Power Station
Provides Helsinki with heating and electricity.

11 Sörnäinen Harbour

12 Transitional periphery
Contains relatively old elements like slaughter-houses and a jail which were originally situated outside the city, as well as temporary storage areas.

13 Hermanni city housing

15 Toukola neighbourhood

(i) **Sanctuary**: Ecology as a collective concern; a holding and preservation scenario.
(ii) **Face of the City**: Helsinki bay area as a city masque.

A Duty Free shopping
Concerns persons coming into the EU and goods to be consumed outside EU boundaries. On purchase one receives a special receipt. On showing the receipt and purchased object, on can claim VAT on leaving the country. There is a duty free shop in the Arabia factory.

B Free storage area
Essentially a piece of neutral ground inside national boundaries meant to temporarily store or exchange transit goods going in and out of the EU without the need to pay duty.

C Intensification of flows
'There is an existing duty free storage area with some assembly functions in Lappeenranta which we are already using. We might be interested if such a proposal could be developed in Helsinki.'
Interview with Valdemar Tretjakov, Moscow Tradehouse in Helsinki

D Influx of new companies
'The biggest hindrance for new companies setting up in Finland is the employee's high income-taxation . . . The aim of such a proposal might be to attract new companies from abroad whose actions are directed to third countries . . . Also exporting creativity rather than goods might be the basis of a company's duty free status.'
Interview with Tapani Kasso, Helsinki Chamber of Commerce

E Tax free zone
'Good connection networks from Finland to St Petersburg make the coastal zone an option for companies considering locating in St Petersburg. The expansion of cross-border networks makes it an attractive alternative.'
The Gulf of Finland coastal zone brochure, 1994

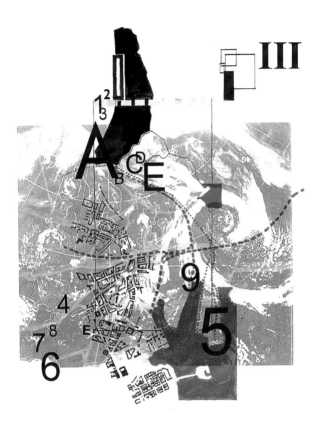

1 **Landowners**
Hackman
Metra
Eläke-Varma

2 **Educational institutions**
UIAH
University of Helsinki, Professor Kari Tikka
Business School

3 **Companies**
Arabia (duty free shop)
Kvaerner Masa-Yards
Spring-offs from UIAH

4 **Local commerce**
Helsinki Chamber of Commerce
Helsinki Met. Development Corporation

5 **International commerce**
Tradehouse of Moscow
Finnish-Russian Trade Association

6 **City of Helsinki**
'The political upheaval in Russia and the Baltic states puts Helsinki in a new geopolitical situation.'
Helsinki City Guide

7 **Finnish government**
Ministry of Employment
Ministry of International Affairs
Taxation

8 **Local people**

9 **Infrastructure**
Highway and harbour proximity

A Existing studies
Model cases: Vladimir, Alexandrov
'Most of the industrial facilities in the city are not in operation (only 20-30% is sustaining) under circumstances of severe competition with foreign companies. Consequently, the city has less tax income for the administrative budget. Just a week ago one of the major factories shut down affecting 10,000 workers and 30,000 families out of the 60,000 population in the city.'
Interview with the Deputy Mayor of Alexandrov, June 10, 1994

B Model of UIAH
Positive impact a new element can have in an institution.

C Stabilisation of boundary
Increased exchange and better knowledge of each other has a clear and long term stabilising effect on uncertain boundaries.

D Intensified networks
Between Russian and Finnish cities and municipalities.

E Common interest
The Institute is beneficial from various points of view, for example, educational and governmental bodies.

F Public awareness
The Institute's work can spread information about Russian conditions to the general public, yet make the studies of an individual researcher more visible.

G Self Organising Municipalities
'There are about 500 self government committees in Moscow at this moment . . . About 300 of them are simplistic, badly educated people, functionaries who are just trying to fight for additional feudal privileges of the precious type of system . . . I know of no more than 15 that combine both higher education, aspiration, will and understanding the fight for their rights. I am afraid we won't succeed immediately. There is no strong support from below.'
V Glazychev, 1994

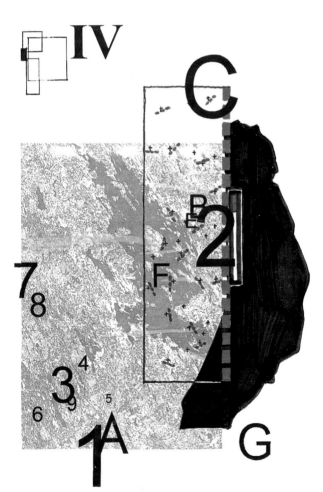

1 **AUE/CHORA**
Academy of Urban Environment in Moscow
CHORA Institute of Architecture and Urbanism

'A school for self-government committees . . . working together with post-graduates, I think would be one of the most creative ways to exchange information. I am ready to a) participate anywhere in the world . . . b) to take people there who would like to work on these issues.'
V Glazychev, founder of AUE, in an interview with Robert Mull, Moscow, June 16, 1994

2 **UIAH**

3 **EU**
Various programmes are possible sources of European Community funding: PACTE, OUVERTURE, ECOS, TARGET, PHARE and TACIS programmes.

4 **The Finnish Government**
'The Ministry of Environment has been supporting environmental programmes in the so-called 'near areas' in Russia and Baltic states.'
Jussi Rautsi

5 **'Friend city' network**

6 **Centre for Urban and Regional Studies (YTK)**
'Interested.'
Mervi Ilmonen

7 **Helsinki University Political Science Department**
'Possibly interested.'
Dept. leader Vilho Harle

8 **The Gulf of Finland Coastal Zone Project**
'I've proposed such an institution but with little success.'
Olli Keinänen, Helsinki City Planning Office

9 **Municipalities in Russia**

(iii) **Urban Trading Floor**: A gateway condition channelling flows of goods and capital.
(iv) **Democratic Urban Regeneration Institution**: Regulation of political stability and migration.

ARABIANRANTA

Chora/Raoul Bunschoten

The application of strategic planning as a game structure, with actors/players, allows for complex urban issues to be dealt with as open-ended generative structures. The game uses difference, conflict and heterogeneity as the necessary prerequisites for catalysing an urban dynamic that ensures its actors must negotiate; a process which requires orchestration or choreography.

Game structures allow complex situations to be modelled using a limited set of rules and a defined game board. Akin to the unfolding of spatial narratives, the game allows negotiated planning to develop as the strategies of each player unfold and interweave, reacting to changing interests and situations.

The production of public space is crucial for the consideration of such complex imperatives, as it is where the various forces, desires and scenarios are played out. The intention is that this organisation will act as a catalyst for an urbanity that is neither fixed nor predetermined.

Four actors and their scenarios – (i) Sanctury, (ii) Face of the City, (iii) Urban Trading Floor and (iv) Democratic Urban regeneration Institution – are proposed, each considered as a type of play linking identity, culture, history and collective memory, allowing interaction. Such an organisation has the potential to be self-regulating, in that, individual desires are kept in check through interaction with other scenarios.

Through the use of such game structures, the site at Arabianranta can be thought of as localizing the concerns of the wider context by weaving larger transformative issues into the local fabric and economies. In this way the site reveals a latent potential that exceeds the scope of the current city plan, and could become a powerful adjunct to the existing centre whilst acting as a gateway to global factors, regulating flows and paradoxically generating the necessary pre-conditions for a complex urbanity.

ABOVE: Scenario (ii) – iconic space
CENTRE: Scenario (iii) – Russian trade
BELOW: Scenario (iii) – bilateral trading across a surface

Key words : alphabet . city . flux . gaming . negotiation . put together

ARCHITECTURE

Dieter Roth

Architecture (regardless of whether they, the architects, erect this or that wherever) is judged by whether you can go into it when you want to go into it, and whether you can go round it when you want to – and even if you can't do what you want to do, it (architecture) is good because it is then good for something, namely for feeling like a child again (as a child you can't always do what you want). Architecture is also judged by whether the people inside (inside the things which they, the architects, have erected) get what they want but the architecture is still good when they don't get it (because once again you feel like a child like in the days when you didn't get all you wanted). And the architecture is also good if it is much too large for you, because then you also feel once more like a child. And when it (the architects' architecture) is too small, it is nevertheless good for making you feel like a child because then the architecture seems like a toy. So whether it is thus or thus, architecture always makes children of everyone, and that is why it is always good.

Key words : flux . play-act

(extract *An Anecdoted Topography of Chance*, 1968)

BASTILLE

Harris Dimitropoulos

A 'monument' for the bicentennial of the storming of the Bastille, Paris, located in the Parc de la Villette; a ritual simulation of the demolition of the building and its dispersal into different house-holds as souvenirs. Twenty-eight towers made of brick and cov-ered in plastic, bearing the inscriptions 'CC' (for the bicentennial) and '*Liberté, Egalité et Fraternité*', were placed in an equilateral triangle, seven on each side referring to the number of prisoners held at the Bastille at the time of the storming. The story of Palloy, the enterprising revolutionary who took the building material pro-duced by the demolition and converted it into souvenirs was included on a plaque next to the monument. The opening cer-emony for the commencement of the demolition was scheduled for the 7th July 1989 and the site remained open to the public for a week. During that time the site/monument was used as a play-ground while the bricks were slowly carried away.

Key words : playground . re-member . territory

BOTTLES, RECYCLE ART PAVILION

Jae-Eun Choi

A conical roof was constructed using 60,000 empty bottles, used as much for their physical attributes (shape, light reflecting quali-ties etc) as for the difficulties they posed for construction; the pavilion appearing as if it is floating in a lake. The building has two levels: the lowest is isolated from all outside light and func-tions as an art gallery, the upper has no function; a space con-sisting of light and material (bottles) only. In the centre of the space is a mirror three metres in diameter. This gathers light and reflects an image of nature outside. This is conceived of as hu-man space, a space, which has no practical function, where use and nature coexist.
[Taejon International Expo, 1993: site area – 2099m²; size – 30x15m; material – 60,000 discarded bottles, glass, hybrid tension struc-ture, concrete and water]

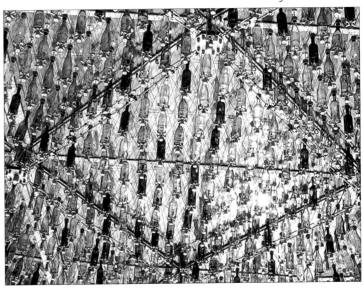

Key words : accumulate . per-form . re-incorporate

BRICKS, REEDY CREEK

VSBA

An emergency services headquarters. Exaggerated in scale, the patterns and colours of red bricks and dalmatian dogs are applied to the exterior of the building which is shaped to reflect the imagery of the traditional American fire station.

[RCID Emergency Services Headquarters, Orlando, Florida. Design architect – Venturi, Scott Brown and Associates, Inc (Principal: Robert Venturi; Project architect: Timothy Kearney, with Steven Izenour, Eva Lew, Amy Noble); Architect – Schenkel Shultz (Principal: J Thomas Chandler; Project manager: Dan Fields; Construction administrator: Gary Krueger)]

Key words : re-presentation . scene . simulate

BRUGES-LA-MORTE, MODEL THEATRE PLAY

Paul Edwards/Ou. Pho. Po

Thirty-five half-tone photographs of the streets and canals of historic Bruges illustrate George Rodenbach's symbolist novel *Bruges-la-Morte*, 1892. The widower Hugues Viane imagines that the town has a personality, that it too is mourning, if it is not the spectre of death itself. The photographs convey this atmosphere: slow shutter speeds have effaced the passers-by, as they have blurred the reflections on the canals. The skies are cloudless and everything appears grey and melancholy. The *Beffroi* (Belfry), with its two holes at the top, looks ominously like a skull. We are made to share Viane's vision as he walks through the streets; we feel we are wandering inside his mental landscape.

In the model theatre play produced by Paul Edwards, the same photographs of the buildings are cut-out and made to move laterally in hidden grooves. The images of Bruges lurch unpredictably, disappearing to the sides or behind each other, lost in the night or veiled in mists. Viane walks the streets in the twilight of morning, and the towers and houses circle him in the shadows of evening. Vistas become silhouettes; blue against a red sky, or red against a blue sky, shiny silver under a grey sky . . .

Hugues has seen a young woman who resembles his dead wife. One day he follows her into a theatre where *Robert le Diable* is being performed. He recognises one of the possessed nuns . . .

The *Beffroi* is about to undergo a terrifying transformation.

Key words : damage . make-believe . pre-tense . psycho-drama . re-make

CHAOS

Jae-Eun Choi

Since 1986, Jae-Eun Choi has carried out an experiment called the 'World Underground Project'. She buries pieces of specially prepared Japanese paper in the ground at random locations around the world. After an extended period of time they are excavated. The paper displays a variety of transformations according to the conditions of each site. After placing the freshly excavated fragments of paper, covered with countless micro-organisms, into an incubator, she magnifies them with a microscope. A miniature universe containing an astonishing degree of diversity emerges. In this exhibition, the viewers looked down at the detailed micro-photographs, fragments of the unknown world beneath their feet, as if peering into a well. This project is a probing of the invisible world inside the soil, rather than the inscription of visible forms into the earth. As Akira Asada stated:

> Beginning with Ilya Prigogine's theory of dissipative structures, chaos and fractal theory show that in an unstable system far from equilibrium the slightest fluctuation has the potential to trigger the process of self-organisation, ultimately creating a new form. Jae-Eun Choi's 'Chaos', while focusing on the world of micro-organisms, is also an allegory of this type of universal principle. It tells us that chaos is precisely what gives birth to our world, allows it to develop, and will cause it to dissipate.
>
> According to Chinese myth, in an attempt to give the featureless face of Chaos literally eyes and a nose, a new hole was dug into its face each day, until finally, when its features were completed, Chaos died. In order to capture chaos, human beings cannot inscribe order into it. Not to represent it to ourselves, but to let it represent itself naturally. In this way, Jae-Eun Choi is attempting to capture living chaos.

['World Underground Project', The Sogetsu Art Museum, Gifu Prefecture, Japan 1991-94]

Key words : ground . hesitation . s pace

CITY

Matt Mullican

Based on charts completed in the mid-70s, Mullican developed the plan of a virtual city, shown for the first time in 1986, after the computer company Digital Editions, Hollywood, placed a computer at his disposal which enabled him to implement the plan over an area of six by three kilometres; subject to scale down to the last detail. Five fundamental levels of consciousness for the appropriation of reality are symbolized by coloured city districts, cut off and yet flowing into one another. Mullican was not interested in animating the design of a Utopian city, merely making a representation of its physical reality. His city is an interpretive space that is made visible by technology. Its entire expanse and urban character exists as a database, only.

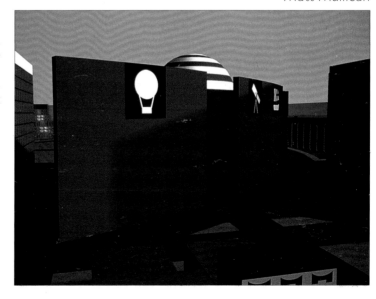

Key words : landscape . playing field . re-presentation

Diller and Scofidio

COMPARED ANATOMY

Joan Fontcuberta

Fontcuberta's work uses the photography of nature as a pretext for investigating the nature of photography. He coined the word 'frottogram' by combining photogram with frottage, an artistic technique proposed by surrealist artist Max Ernst. Frottograms were intended to be a means by which the superficial structure of objects could be directly transferred onto paper, in much the same way as a photographer creates a photogram by placing objects (rather than negatives) directly onto photographic paper. In these frottograms a negative of a rock, plant, animal or fragment of the human body is rubbed against that same object. The final print contains a dual representation of the object – both visual and physical. In the self-portraits featured here, parts of the artist's mouth and chin are spliced together with images of a wax model and other physiological diagrams. Few familiar facial landmarks survive this process, the combination of scratched negative, bearded chin and yawning orifice is at once terrifyingly explicit and peculiarly distant.

Key words : characterize . friction . damage . recall

CROTON AQUEDUCT

RAAUm

The site of this ongoing study is located along the New York City water supply infrastructure; a branching linear system of reservoirs, aqueducts and tunnels which stretches from rural upstate New York to the dense network of city water mains.

We saw the route of the aqueduct as a device for opening up questions about the local history of the places through which it travels. We mapped the entire length of the system and recorded every street and road that the aqueduct crossed. This gave us a drawing on which to locate interventions and invent programs in response to the place names.

Michel de Certeau has written, in *The Practice of Everyday Life*, about the uncanny persistence of meaning in place names:

> Disposed in constellations that hierarchize and semantically order the surface of the city, operating chronological arrangements and historical justifications, these words (the street names) slowly lose, like worn coins, the value engraved on them, but their ability to signify outlives its first definitions . . . a strange toponymy that is detached from actual places and flies high over the city like a foggy geography of 'meanings' held in suspension, directing the physical perambulations below.

This 'foggy geography of meanings', a semantic surplus encoded in place names, seemed a productive device to generate programs with a distinct connection to the place as well as a detachment allowing for invention and critique. De Certeau proposes a specifically political reading of this condition:

> Linking acts and footsteps, opening meanings and directions, these words operate in the name of an emptying out and wearing away of their primary role. They become liberated spaces which can be occupied. A means of a semantic rarefication, rich in determination, the function of articulating a second, poetic geography on top of the literal, forbidden or permitted meaning. They insinuate other routes into the functionalist and historical order of movement.

(Stan Allen)

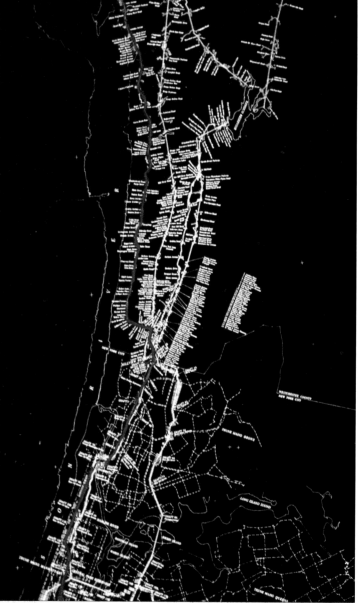

Key words : field geography . warning

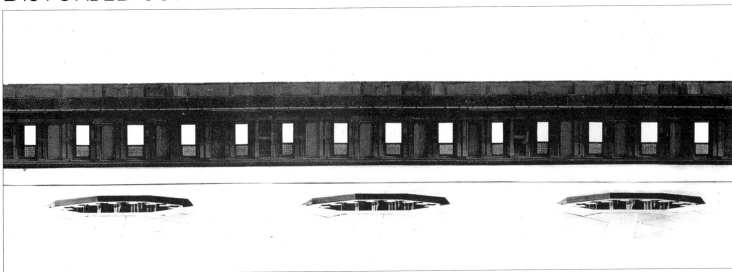

Key words : deception . re-creation

FIELD CONDITIONS

Stan Allen

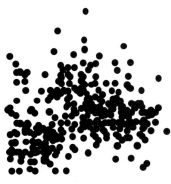

We will designate a 'field condition' any formal or spatial matrix capable of unifying diverse elements while respecting the identity of each. Field configurations are loosely bounded aggregates characterized by porosity and local interconnectivity. The internal regulations of the parts are decisive; overall shape and extent are highly fluid. Field conditions are bottom-up phenomena; defined not by overarching geometrical schemata but by intricate local connections. Interval, repetition and seriality are key concepts. Form matters, but not so much the form of things as the form between things.

By comparison with western classical architecture, it is possible to identify contrasting principles of combination; one algebraic, working with numerical units combined one after another, and the other geometric, working with figures (lines). Aggregated, processional space, typical of both classical and modernist composition, gives way to a non-directional space, a serial order of 'one thing after another'.

Field conditions cannot claim (does not intend to claim) to produce a systematic theory of architectural form or composition. The theoretical model proposed here anticipates its own irrelevance in the face of the realities of practice. These are working concepts, derived from experimentation, in contact with the real. Field conditions intentionally mix high theory with low practice. The assumption here is that architectural theory does not arise in a vacuum, but always in a complex dialogue with practical work. Field conditions treats constraints as opportunity, and moves away from a modernist ethic – and aesthetics – of transgression. Working with and not against the site, something new is produced by registering the complexity of the given.

ABOVE, LEFT to RIGHT: Scatter; KOMA roof; BELOW: Weave + striation

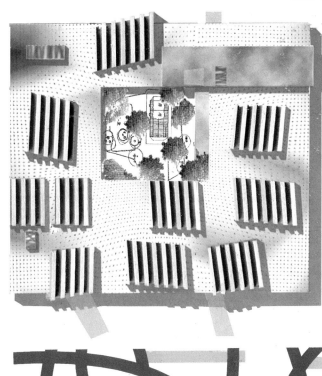

Key words : field . geography . negotiation

FLATSCAPE

Abbot, EA – Flatland.

BIG SKY,

Construction, never complete

Datascape

Erasure, never complete

Fields of ideographs –

GHOSTS:

History as hallucination,

Islands of Maximum Displacement.

Junk,

Kitsch,

Light; 24 hours – no stopping.

MOTORWAYS – no stopping.

New articulations of surface – new effects –

Over-exposed

Palimpsests (on which the game of identity and relation is perpetually rewritten),

Quotidian

REMAINS.

Scenery (*keshiki*) + Skyscape (*kuukei*),

Text space,

Unexpected social spaces,

Violence,

Webs of connection,

EXCESS

Yielding

Zones of Maximum Potential

Example: Brent Cross, North London, where the terrain has been changing continuously since the mid-19th century. The Town and Country Planning Acts of the 1940s had a profound impact on the suburban character of the area, and proximity to Heathrow airport and the M1 motorway has stimulated large-scale ribbon-development along the major roads. This area is now being re-formed into cluster arrangements where shopping and entertainment zones, hotels and business parks cohabit with inter-war and post war suburban housing, the remaining 19th-century infrastructure and new high-speed roads; a zone of maximum potential.
Key words : continuous change . e-scape . flatness . land

FLOODED CITY

Algorithm:
Put object [ ] in water and see what happens.
Put object in water where [ ] = pencils.

Reference 1:
The custom of throwing gifts into wishing wells, the wish maker making a silent wish.

Reference 2:
Le Monde 16th January 1995; 'An overflow floods and washes the city . . . the inundation develops a dynamic of solidarity; with it the euphoria of reconstructing the quarter, giving it new roads, using it as a theatrical space.'

a. The hand throws the [object] pencils – the surface of the water opens, a motion of the hand, the pencils fall.

Holding with full hand, vertical pencils, let go, pencils fall.
Holding with two fingers, two pencils, let go, pencils fall.
Holding with three fingers, three pencils, let go, pencils fall.
Holding with four fingers, four pencils, let go, pencils fall.
Holding with full hand, horizontal pencils, let go, pencils fall.

(Their encounter with the hand stays behind.)

Water moves.

b. Garden: thin squirts, splashes, washes, gushes, murmurs. Plugged with leaves or fingers the garden stutters, quenches the sober.

c. Potential form: Point Carré Fountain.

Point: transparent room, 1x4m, white water (emptying out or filling), constant movement.
Carré: transparent room, 5x5x4m, bodies (emptying out or filling), constant movement, white water affects, diverse colouring, white water effects.
Inondata: shallow basin, 23x13m, surface patterns, texture, white water; from almost empty to overflowing.
Four Rivers Park: two rivers with double sources and one well, two rivers with a single source and one well, vegetation, crystals, valley, dry land, wet land, voice gardens.

A clear and pure voice with running words, singing drop by drop.

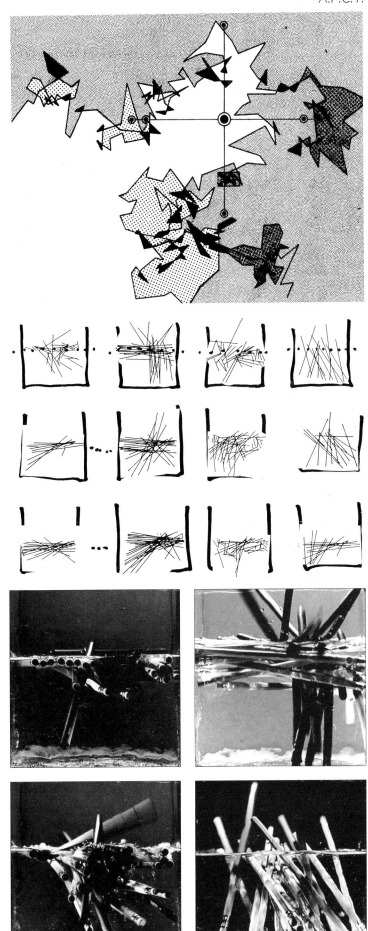

Key words : algorithm . repetition . wave motion

GAMES OF LOVE AND CHANCE

JEROME SANS – The contemporary world is witnessing a great evolution of the society of leisure. With home shopping, Pay TV, video games and virtual reality, we are developing a fully-fledged aesthetics of play.

PAUL VIRILIO – *Two attitudes are possible with respect to these new technologies: the first declares them a miracle; the second – mine – recognizes that they are interesting while maintaining a critical attitude. The imminent home installation of domestic simulators and virtual space rooms for game playing poses many questions, and in particular this one: 'What is a game once the virtual invades reality?' There are two ways of understanding the notion of play – playing-cards, dominoes, checkers – or the play of a mechanical part when it is loose in its housing. I think, in fact, that the second is the angle from which we should envision play today. Play is not something that brings pleasure; on the contrary, it expresses a shift in reality, an unaccustomed mobility with respect to reality. To play today, in a certain sense, means to choose between two realities. A concrete factual reality: meet someone, love that person, make love to that person. Or the game reality: use the technologies of cybersex to meet that person from a distance, without touching or risk of contamination, contact without contact. What is at play in this case is an illness different from that associated with traditional games and provoked by chance. Gamblers can't do with out chance, they are addicted to it and can't break the habit. I believe that alongside those addicted to chance, to roulette, to cards or to any game, a new kind of addict is being born: the addict of the virtual. People will become hooked on virtuality and will find themselves in an awkward position, torn between two realities. We can already see it on Wall Street and in the stock markets; the casinos where 'traders' or 'golden boys' play with the virtuality of international markets which are increasingly disconnected from the economic reality of the world.*

It's a kind of electronic addiction which leads to a virtual addiction.

– You could say that drugs are a game people get 'hooked' on. Those who are addicted to card games or the roulette table always end up playing Russian roulette. Games and death, games and accidents, are related. When you play at chance, you are compelled to play and thus no longer free to play; a physical or mental death occurs. Now video games, or the more sophisticated games of tomorrow's virtual reality, will induce this same desire for death. A desire to cross the boundary. I am not a big player. What interests me today in the state of play is cybersex, because it seems to be the most extraordinary aspect of social deregulation. In addition to today's divorce epidemic – which can be attributed to other things than a lack of morality (I'm not playing the moralist here) – another type of divorce is brewing. Instead of living together, people now live apart. An example of this (without cybersex, but in an atmosphere that cybersex will cultivate) is the student couple who invited me to their wedding and after the ceremony went home separately. They told me, 'This way we stay free.' 'That's great,' I said, 'your children won't be shocked if you get divorced one day because they'll have divided their time between your two homes anyway.' Cybersex pushes this logic even farther. It's not divorce, it's the disintegration of the couple. You don't make love anymore because it's dangerous, because sometimes there are problems; one person may not be very skilled or the situation may get messy. So you use a kind of machine, a machine that transfers physical and sexual contact by waves. What is at play is no longer the connector rod in its housing, but the loss of what is most intimate in our experience of the body. The actor Louis Jouvet wrote, 'Everything is suspect, except the body and its

sensations.' From now on, with virtuality and electronic copulation, even the body and its sensations will be suspect. In cybersex, one sees, touches and smells. The only thing one can't do is taste the other's saliva or semen. It's a 'super-condom'.

The sociologist Michel Maffesoli speaks of the development of 'neo-tribalism', a desire to regroup, through all the possibilities of long-distance communication. It seems, nonetheless, that we are still dealing with an experience of solitary satisfaction.

– I don't believe in a return of tribes, and I don't think that a gang is a tribe. As I said in my book L'Inertie Polaire, *what's on its way is the planet man, the self-sufficient man who, with the help of technology, no longer needs to reach out to others because others come to him. With cybersexuality, he doesn't need to make love at his partner's house, love comes to him instantly, like a fax or a message on the electronic highway. The future lies in cosmic solitude. I picture a weightless individual in a little ergonomic armchair, suspended outside a space capsule, with the earth below and the interstellar void above. A man with his own gravity, who no longer needs a relationship to society, to those around him and least of all to a family. Maffesoli's tribalisation is a totally outmoded vision; the future lies in an unimaginable solitude – of which play is one element.*

One has the impression that the player's quest ends in a narcissistic orgasm.

– Yes, but it's a narcissism that is expanding.

Some go so far as to say that video games mark a modern triumph of the icon.

*– Those are the thaumaturgists, the miracle-criers. You have to be extremely wary of what the critic Jacques Ellul called 'the technological bluff'. Today we have admen, even experts, who spend all their time saying how wonderful technology is. They are giving it the kiss of death. By being critical I do more for the development of new technologies than by giving in to my illusions and refusing to question technology's negative aspects. When the railroad was invented, so was derailment. Then there were people like me who said right away that they didn't care if trains were great and went faster than stagecoaches. What was more important was that they (did) not derail, that the accident specific to the train (did) not prevent its development. These people worked on the problems of railroad accidents and invented the 'block system' for signalling, which has made the TGV (*Train à Grande Vitesse, *a French express train capable of travelling at over 230km per hour) possible in France. The same can be said for aviation and so on. The accidents of virtual reality, of telecommunications, are infinitely less visible than derailments, but they are potentially just as serious. And there will be no block system as long as we listen to the prophets of joy.*

Video games have an incredibly imaginative side, a marvellous narrative, a journey through which the player can be transformed into a hero.

– This is crucial. In writing societies, the narrative is the journey. The first line of Moby Dick, *'Call me Ishmael', sets the story in motion, begins Ishmael's journey. In writing, the narrative carries you along. On screen it's the visual rather than descriptive simulation of a voyage (along tracks, through a labyrinth, through a tunnel) that moves you. Thus the simulator becomes the new*

novel, the virtual journey replaces the poetic quality of the story, whether it be The Arabian Nights *or* Ulysses.

So the new player is a traveller.

— *Yes. But now the travellers are travelled; dreamers are dreamed. They are no longer free to move about, they are travelled by the programme. They are no longer free to dream, they are dreamed by the programme.*

This player is a hero in a hurry.

— *He's a man hurried by the machine. Mental images are replaced by mechanical instruments. Reading, one fabricates a mental cinema; each of us sees a different Madame Bovary at her window. In the Bovary video game, there will be only one Madame Bovary, the one in the programme.*

We're getting back to your old hobby-horse: the idea that images are weapons.

— *Cybersex is really the civil war of sex, since people are divided by it. More sophisticated games could replace society altogether. Aren't poles — electronic democracy, in a sense — electronic games which are replacing political reality?*

What difference is there between video games and the simulations produced by war programmes?

— *As I wrote in* L'Ecran du Desert *(my chronicle of the Gulf War), many strategists said that it was easier to understand the Gulf War by buying American video games than by watching the news on television. In a certain sense, they were right. We didn't see concrete events — how the ground troops broke through the Iraqi border for example — but we did see war transformed into a video game, with the same image repeated over and over; a weapon hitting its target. That image is still very present.*

The division of perception into two realities causes a blurring comparable to intoxication: we are seeing double. It's impossible to imagine what this will ultimately produce several generations down the road. To live in one reality and then, from time to time, enter another — through a night of drinking or hallucinogens — is one thing, but to live all the time through telecommunications and the electronic highway is another. I don't think we can even imagine what it may provoke in people's minds and in society to live constantly with this 'stereo-reality'. It is absolutely without precedent.

Faced with the plethora of possibilities, what game should we play?

— *Play at being a critic. Deconstruct the game in order to play with it. Instead of accepting the rules, challenge and modify them. Without the freedom to criticize and reconstruct, there is no truly free game; we are addicts and nothing more.*

Key words : foreplay . friction . play . trick

(translated by Carol Volk)

Arakawa and Madeline Gins

The critical, ironic stance requires the taking of things to heart as much as does any other stance; it requires perhaps a double taking of things to heart. God (ungendered)

So that life might be ample, take things to heart as much as possible, but remember that taking things too much to heart will destroy you. God (androgynous)

The fate of each 'I' is sealed by that which surrounds it. In the sentence 'I am a person', it is not only the word 'I', but all four words or concepts of the sentence taken together that give 'I' its meaning. In addition to this, the 'I' receives support from all sentences and concepts within which the speaker/reader has found 'I' to be active or has believed it to be embedded. Embedding (words infiltrating each other), the division of linguistic labour (language not as the possession of a single speaker but as a co-operative activity; terms cannot be defined in isolation, each word holds a part of the meaning) and holism (all sentences have a say in the resultant meaning) as working principles of language bolster the stand-up sliver or slip of an 'I'.

Despite massive shoring up, the 'I' can readily be undermined, as Arthur Rimbaud's amazing equation demonstrates in a flash: '*Je suis un autre.*'

'I have met the other and that other is myself of yesterday as well as the "me of today".'

'Do you wish to express an estrangement from the smell of your own intimate me?'

'Nothing is closer to my (that is the other's) heart!'

'Who or what is this other to which or to whom you impute your very self?'

'Any other will do.'

* * *

'What does the other want?'

'The other wants to persist as me!'

'Which me!'

'The other more expandable, less caved in me!'

The purpose of architecture is to sculpt the other, although most architects are unaware of this. Architecture exists to sculpt the other into a long and longer life. Architecture should provide circumstances that allow the other to sculpt the length of its own existence as an 'I'. Let architecture reek of the other.

What needs to be done to effect this?

Configure the landing sites in their mechanicalness to refurbish sensibility.

In the case of the first site of reversible destiny the other finds itself in central Japan. Here is the Japan of your otherness.
A 122m Japan outlined by cement and filled with sprawling herb gardens straddles the entire elliptical bowl. Nearby, at right angles to it, lies a 45m cement Japan painted silver. A 1.8m topo-graphical map of Japan sits on a mound on the outer face of the steep slope at the bowl's edge. Underground within the bowl, far tinier Japans surface as nothing but light and air. Everywhere one looks Japan lies ready to be found. Japan, the island-chain nation, loses its singularity becoming instead only one of several similarly configured sets of landing sites, each of which readily accepts, even begs for, the designation Japan. The most 'real' of all the configurations of landing sites that add up to a 'Japan', the actual Japan, the land, the island-chain and the nation, upon and within which the whole slew of variously scaled other Japans sit, paradoxically enough turns out to be the one that is, at least in its contours, the most invisible of all!

One Japan subverts, or supplants, another and the co-ordinating of landing sites becomes discordant. Japan in profusion, a superabundance of references, threatens to erase position through over-determination.

Within these surroundings, the question 'Where are you?' readily translates into 'What goes into (or participates in) your determining of where you are?' A divided loyalty to position becomes thinkable, or at least noticeable, and the architecture motivates a complex response to a whole set of what were once, but no longer are, difficult-to-comprehend questions. As for what goes into the determining of where one is, the universal reply would more or less add up to: 'The group of everything that I hold in place is determinative of where I judge myself to be. For example, I form Japan out of all that I hold in place as Japan. Japan is/are a group.' Asked 'How is Japan sited' or 'How have you sited it?' or, more in keeping with the present terminology, 'Where have you landed' or 'Where are you landing?' the reply of virtually every visitor to the first site of reversible destiny would convey chiefly this: 'In part here, in part there, in part everywhere within my perceptual ken.'

Mounds like those situated within the elliptical bowl are placed both on the surrounding slopes at one end and atop the high wall at the other. These raised mounds mediate the distance. Visitors will associate them both with the rounded caps of Yoro mountain and the mounds sitting within the bowl. Artificially raised above the earth and positioned neither here nor there, even though they are certainly where they are, these mounds, in any event, belong to Japan and represent yet another degree of it. And the sky too at this juncture? – yet another degree of Japan?

Under investigation here is everything, every entity, event and site that goes into the determination of where one is. Holding open one's positioning of oneself, keeping it in abeyance, allows for regrouping. As demonstrated above, not only is/am 'I' an other, 'I' am/is/are also a group, with now this surfacing, now that surfacing as me, as my other.

Each neighbourhood is designed to redirect the co-ordinating of landing sites in a distinctive way, so as to be a unique approach to a holding open and re-distributing of the world as formed and forming. Streets within the section known as **Elsewhere** and **Not** are named contrary to that which is the case for those who traverse them. Named in contradistinction to where they are in relation to those setting foot on them and so never able to be successfully landed upon as what or where they purport to be, they propel whoever visits them constantly ever onward, always elsewhere. In a few cases, instead of presenting visitors with information not jibing with the facts, street names in this section serve up blatant non-truths. In the section known as the **Body Enclave**, street names appeal more directly to the body than to the person, but it is the other way around in the **Person Region**. Street names in the **Person as World Suffusion Zone** alert a visitor to how determinative – of the world in which she finds herself – is that which constitutes her as a person; the sum of each and every one of her actions. Street names within the **Neutralized and Neutralizing Delta** encourage a neutralizing of subjectivity. The above-mentioned areas and the following ones as well – **Landing Site Processing Zone, All Here and There Village,**

Voice Plaza, Scale Adjustment Zone and **Reversible Destiny Re-doubled Effort Zone** – help visitors elude the defeatism of a thus-far universal belief in the inevitability of death and guide them toward working out a viable reversible destiny.

Every one of our streets might have been named 'This Street' to a different effect. Where are you now? I am on 'This Street', but only a moment before I moved along a completely different 'This Street'; 'This' as a name affixed to a street derails the language-game of proper names. There might be a 'This or That Street' that could be taken either way depending on where one was situated, but failing that, if the rules of naming are to be followed, no 'This Street' can be correctly pointed out as a 'That Street' despite the urgent demand that grammar would seem to put on one to do so. What might be permissible would be to allude to a 'that "This Street"', as in, 'I was skipping along on that "This Street" prior to having arrived on "This Street".'

A thoroughgoing naming of streets with 'This' and only 'This' as a chosen name might lead to descriptive sequences such as the following: 'Here I am on 'This Street'. I'll turn off it at this point and go down 'This Street'. 'This Street', my third 'This Street' in this sequence, is far more demanding of my attention than the first two were.'

A name this general, applied ubiquitously, foregrounds the shape, angle and the position of what is being named (the paths). Naming in this way also highlights the body as it is experiencing the path, the forms the body assumes in response to what 'This Street' puts before it. Each 'This Street' has its own explanation.

Alternatively, all our streets marked 'This Street' might be taken as an all in one 'This Street' that, traversing the whole of the site, at times breaks off, but remains re-connectable, re-connecting, unitary. In this interpretation as well, the special features of each turn in the path would come to the fore, doing most of the 'talking' thanks to the self-effacing nature of the name.

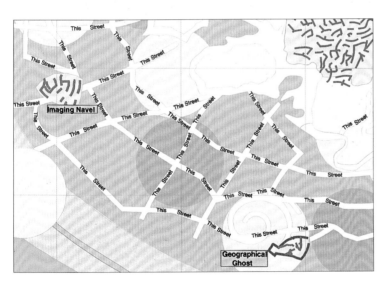

The above case of street naming exemplifies a refusal to use words to make distinctions even as the naming process continues. In the following example, along with a refusal to make distinctions, comes a stated contradiction scheduled to detonate each time the reader/walker sets foot on the street. The naming process permits, in some sense, a walker to tread where prior to such naming she never could; it enables her to stroll through the heretofore impossible region of the 'here yonder'.

But the avowed wish is to arrive at a reversing of destiny. How then to punch holes – black holes, writhing holes, source holes, Blake holes, replete holes – into mortality? Sieve mortality and stop it. Begin by punching holes in the referring process.

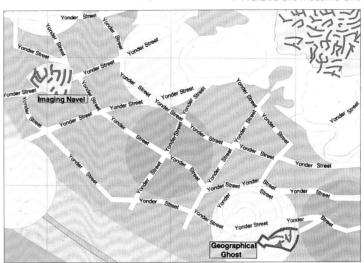

'Pardon me, what is it you are referring to?'

'I am not referring to how to live forever, only to come to a rude and abrupt end!'

* * *

Doom: the 'natural' conclusion of a 'real' life is said to be death. All death is mortal.

To be human is be mortal; to be human is to err. Death is a reference that flaps in the breeze. Next subject.

'Excuse me, I don't quite know where I am. Could you tell me what street I'm on?'

'Of course. You're on "Afar Street".'

'Really? Well, where does that get me? Or, what a relief not to have to be where I am. Or, I bite the distance.'

'And did you say you would wait for me on "Only Street"?'

'Granted it is not the only street in the vicinity and yet it is the only one on which I expect to meet you, never mind that it is only a street.'

Only: a jot of, a jutting out of, the stuff of, the only universe, holding its own as a landing site.

'All that you take to heart will be taken from you!'

The only streets worth standing on are those set up to guide the body to construct a world in different terms from this. The body in person is a co-ordinator of, a juggler of, landing sites. Moving along humble, little 'Only Street', the body will learn many of the intricacies involved in the co-ordinating of landing sites. Until one day, when strolling along another street, one that is also only what it is, one perhaps named, yes, for example, 'Anti-Cemetery Lane', the body as a person will in some definitive way be found to have at last escaped the wrath of God, that is 'God'. The universe could not ask for more, at least not prior to there having been such an escape.

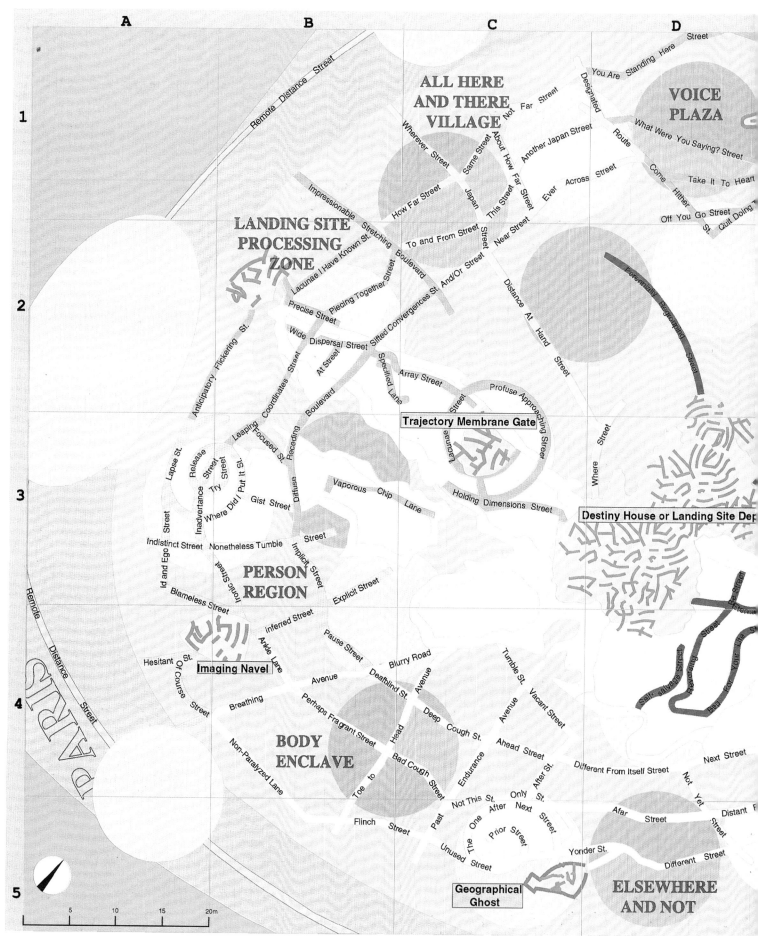

THE GAME BOTH BEGINS AND IS OVER, OR TRANSMUTES INTO A NON-GAME, ONCE THE REG-

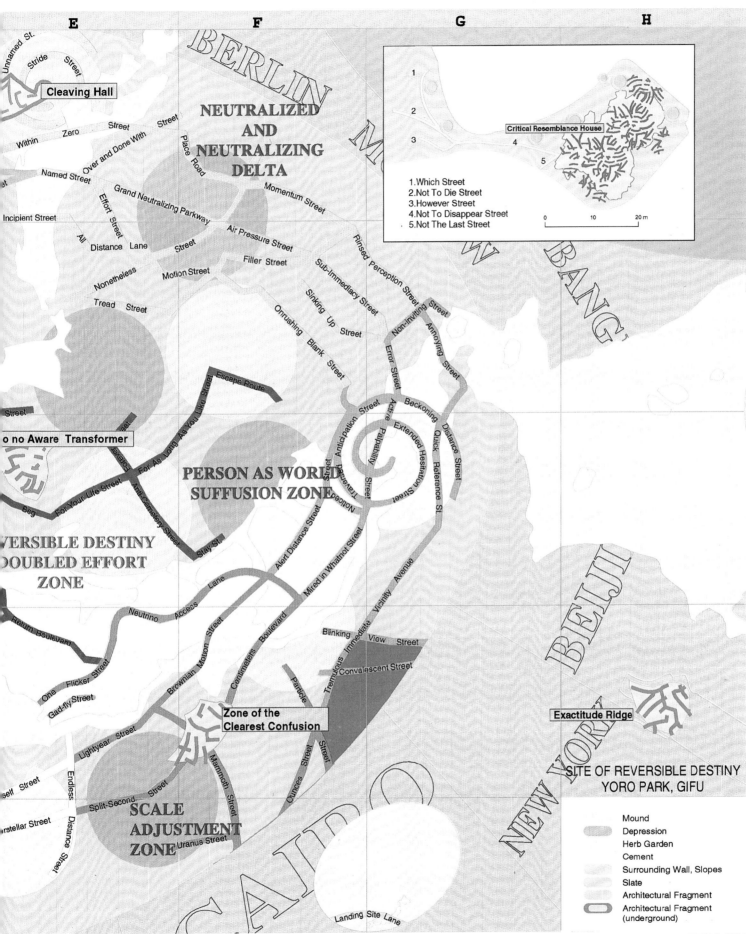

E   **F**   **G**   **H**

Unnamed St.

Stride Street

Cleaving Hall

Zero Street Street

Within Over and Done With

Named Street

Incipient Street

Effort Street

Grand Neutralizing Parkway

All Distance Lane

Street

Nonetheless Motion Street

Tread Street

Street

o no Aware Transformer

For As Long As You Like Line Street

Beg For Your Life Street Ann Cemetery Street

Escape Route

VERSIBLE DESTINY
DOUBLED EFFORT
ZONE

Stay St.

Neutrino Access

Return Boulevard

One Flicker Street

Gad-fly Street

Lightyear Street

elf Street Endless

Split-Second Street Mammoth Street

rstellar Street Distance Street

**SCALE
ADJUSTMENT
ZONE** Uranus Street

NEUTRALIZED
AND
NEUTRALIZING
DELTA

Place Road

Momentum Street

Air Pressure Street

Filler Street

Sub-Immediacy Street

Rinsed Perception Street

Sinking Up Street

Onrushing Blank Street

Non-Inviting Street

Annoying Street

Error Street

Noticeable Anticipation Street

Active Palpability Street

Extended Hesitation Street

Beckoning Street

Quick Reference St.

Distance Street

**PERSON AS WORLD
SUFFUSION ZONE**

Traversed Street

Alert Distance Street

Lane

Mired in Whatnot Street

Centimeters Boulevard

Brownian Motion Street

Particle Street

Blinking Immediate View Street

Tremulous Vicinity Avenue

Convalescent Street

Ounces Street

Street

**Zone of the
Clearest Confusion**

Landing Site Lane

BERLIN

MOW BANG

BEIJI NEW YORK

CAIRO

Exactitude Ridge

**SITE OF REVERSIBLE DESTINY
YORO PARK, GIFU**

Inset (top right):

1   2   3   4   5

Critical Resemblance House

0   10   20 m

1. Which Street
2. Not To Die Street
3. However Street
4. Not To Disappear Street
5. Not The Last Street

Legend:

- Mound
- Depression
- Herb Garden
- Cement
- Surrounding Wall, Slopes
- Slate
- Architectural Fragment
- Architectural Fragment (underground)

IONAL APPROACHES TO (THE SECURING OF A) REVERSIBLE DESTINY HAVE BEEN DETERMINED

TYPES OF FUNCTION:

FOR HUMAN (SUPER-)COMFORT
Le Corbusier . Villa Savoye . 1931

Arakawa and Madeline Gins

FOR THE SAKE OF UNIVERSAL SPACE-TIME
Mies van der Rohe . Farnsworth House . 1951

FOR THE SAKE OF THE BODY
FOR DETERMINING THE SITE OF A PERSON
Arakawa + Madeline Gins . Critical Resemblance House . 1995

Instructions for use (to be continued)
The Elliptical Field

• Instead of being fearful of losing your balance, look forward to it (as a desirable reordering of the landing sites, formerly known as the senses).

• When moving through the **Elliptical Field** remember as many views of the **Critical Resemblance House** as possible, and vice versa.

• Try to draw the sky down into the bowl of the field.

• Use each of the five Japans to locate, or compose, where you are.

• Always question where you are in relation to the visible and invisible chains of islands known as Japan.

To secure a sense of yourself as this site (the entire elliptical field):

• Vary the rate at which you move through it.

• Associate each of the extreme forms your body is forced to assume in traversing it with both a nearby and a distant form.

• If accidentally thrown completely off balance, try to note the number, and also the type and placement, of the landing sites essential to reconstituting a world.

• Frequently swing round to look behind you.

• Minimize the number of focal areas (perceptual landing sites) at any given moment.

• If an area or a landing site catches your eye and attracts your interest to the same degree as the area through which you are actually moving, take it up on the spot, pursuing it as best you can as a parallel zone of activity.

• Make use of the **Exactitude Ridge** to register each measured sequence of events that makes up the distance.

• Within the **Zone of the Clearest Confusion** always try to be more body and less person.

• To make a decision or to become more subtle or daring, or both, in regard to a previous decision, use the **Mono no Aware Transformer**.

• Inside the **Geographical Ghost** renege on all geographically related pledges of allegiance.

• Wander through the ruin known as the **Destiny House** or the **Landing Site Depot** as though you were an extraterrestrial.

• Move in slow measured steps through the **Cleaving Hall** and, with each arm at a distinctly different height, hold both arms out in front of you as sleepwalkers purportedly do.

• Close your eyes when moving through and around the **Trajectory Membrane Gate**.

• In and about the **Kinesthetic Pass**, repeat every action two or three times, once in slow motion.

• Walk backwards in and near the **Imaging Navel**.

The Critical Resemblance House

• Enter the house several times, each time through a different entrance.

• If thrown off balance when entering the house, call out your name or, if you prefer, someone else's.

• Strive to find a marked resemblance between yourself and the house. If by chance you fail to do so, proceed as if the house were your identical twin.

• Move through the house as though you were presently living in it, or as though you were its next resident.

• Should an unexpected event occur, freeze in place for as long as you see fit. Then adopt a more suitable (or more thought out) position for an additional 20 seconds or so.

    Perceptual Landing Site: any discerning of any event whatsoever.
    Imaging Landing Site: any filling in of the gaps between/among perceptual landing sites.
    Architectural Landing Site: any registering of dimension/position.

• Try to incorporate two or more horizons into every view.

• Use each set of furniture as a concrete reference for the other sets.

• Search out identical moments in segments of the house that are remote from one another. Attempt this initially with strikingly similar configurations, and eventually with widely divergent ones.

Key words : judgement . no-place . place . without judgement

GLOBE THEATRE, ENGENDERING PLATE

Reiser and Umemoto

I had built-up a papier mâché hemisphere from alternate layers of Yellow Pages and newsprint. As I began sanding the inevitable irregularities that covered the surface of the newly made form, the higher areas were naturally removed first; obliterating the language from that layer and revealing the language of the underlying layers. The resulting surface, criss-crossed with miscellaneous bits of language and fortuitous conjunctions, had the appearance of a terrestrial globe.

I began to play with the idea that the act of sanding was in some way analogous to the action of a catalyst which promotes a reaction but itself remains unchanged and indifferent. The emergence of new combinations of word fragments likewise proceeded only as long as the sanding action continued. When the sanding ceased, the configurations would then be fixed just as live bacteria are fixed on slides before viewing.

A 28x43cm portion of the engendering plate was enlarged photographically to 42x62.5cm to enhance its readability, and was then divided into 4cm squares, as in a Mercator's projection. The vertical axis was lettered from A-K and the horizontal axis numbered from 1-17 creating 181 squares or views. Subsequent operations on each view were performed in isolation from the adjacent images. It was found that most squares produced three legible bits of language, which were recorded in a book set-up for this process; cataloguing each view and three salient pieces of language or 'residents'. The next series of operations utilized a five by five matrix: the 'martial gridiron'. The letters of the alphabet (not including the letter z) were shuffled and then chosen at random to be affixed within each square of the grid; the letter z was dropped outside the field as a foil to the grid's determinacy. The letters of the residents were then plotted into their respective locations within the grid and connected with lines; starting with the first letter of the resident and continuing to the last.

The martial grid cuts open, as with a sword, the language of the resident revealing an internal sign or signature. Each figure was then duly recorded in the book alongside its corresponding resident, creating a total of 561.

(Jesse Reiser)

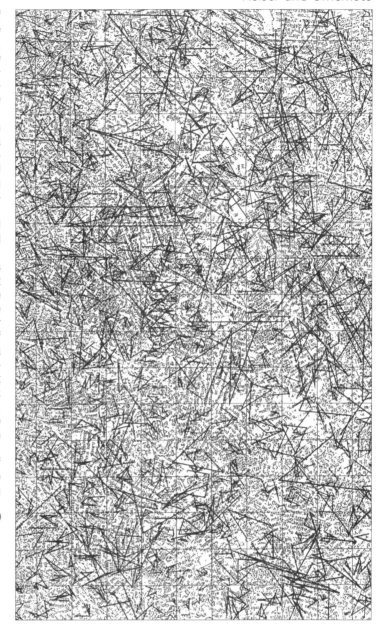

Key words : alphabet . connection . repetition . writing

GLYPHS

Dream work on datascapes: mining the depthless space of information; a pure erotic project.

Implosion: in a world that (no longer) makes sense; a world filled with text, numbers – data pollution, excessive but opaque, an immense 'combinatoria' – condensation must be taking place on a large-scale. The only logical relationship being 'just as', constructed according to similarity, consonance, regression to the diagram, to the mark, to the trace; or advancing from the track, to the mark (seeds; more detailed than the trace) to the diagram, the design (imaged forms; pictograms, designations of situations, associative complexes, ideographs with multiple significations, the speech of weaving[1]); fragments not just held together but compressed, intensively reduced and accelerated. Condensation is not based on omission but is more like a nodal point upon which a great number of (dream) thoughts converge.

Freud considered the extremely condensed signs of the symbolism of dreams analogous to hieroglyphs:

> . . . it is fair to say that the productions of the dream work which, it must be remarked, are not made with the intention of being understood, present no greater difficulties to their translators than do the ancient hieroglyphic scripts to those who seek to read them.[2]

The symbols of dreams;

> . . . frequently have more than one or even several meanings, and, as with Chinese script, the correct interpretation can only be arrived at on each occasion from the context. The ambiguity of the symbols links up with the characteristic of dreams for admitting 'over-interpretation' – for representing in a single piece of content thoughts and wishes often widely divergent in nature.[3]

The seduction of non-alphabetic writing.

NOTES

1 Julia Kristeva, *Language, The Unknown*, trans Anne M Menke, Columbia University Press, (New York)1989, p61.

2 Sigmund Freud, *The Interpretation of Dreams*, ed James Strachey, Penguin,(London) 1976, p457.

3 Ibid, p470.

Key words : carving . datascape . dream . hieroglyph

GOOSE GAME

'*Jeu de L'oie – Jeu de Loi, Strategies Urbaines Pour Ilots Insalubres de Menilmontant et Belleville*' a work in progress; a mixture of delirium and realism, operating in a minor mode to save the existing urban fabric.

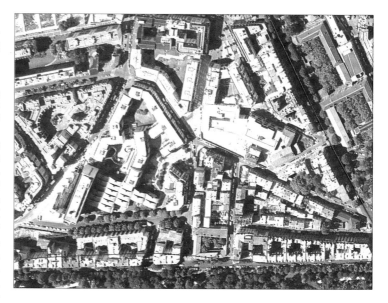

In order to elaborate an urban renovation plan, Claire Robinson, American architecture professor, has divided the neighbourhood into sixty-three parcels corresponding to as many architects who are working on them from the United States.

On Friday night, the top floor of the factory at 49 rue des Partants (*XXe arrondissement*) glowed within the obscurity of the last part of the ZAC des Amandiers, which is destined for demoli-

tion and whose occupants are threatened with eviction. In this space, which is also its headquarters, the association Archi XX inaugurated 'The Goose Game – Law Game' exhibition; otherwise known as the 'Urban Strategies for Insalubrious Islands in Menilmontant and Belleville'. Here the residents' lawyers, local representatives of the Communist Party, Socialist Party and Green Party, diverse neighbourhood defence associations and fans of architecture responded in mass to the invitation of the American Claire Robinson; initiator of this audacious adventure begun three years earlier.

'Last September's exhibition was to ascertain what was necessary to continue. Next October, we would like to propose an urban plan', commented the American while making a tour through the plans, models, photographs and sketches of 'The Goose Game – Law Game'. This exhibition concentrates on the first stage of work, an X-ray of the neighbourhood, including an analysis of the remaining buildings and the history of the inhabitants. Claire Robinson explained the future in the following terms: 'the ZAC is divided into 63 parcels. Each one is entrusted to an architect who works for example on the renovation of an existing building. We need 63 players, we have 50 at the moment. We contact each other regularly by fax to keep an overview.'

An invitation to dream

On the wall the first sketches of renovation already mingle with social documents, family photographs, furniture and objects. The inhabitants of the actual buildings which are uncomfortable due to the lack of maintenance come to the exhibit to dream, noses to the wall, staring at the barely hatched models. One rare apartment 'owner' prefers to complain. She explains that she would rather take expropriation indemnities and disappear forever from the neighbourhood. Everybody has a point of view. Near the exit an old Moroccan is sitting cloaked in his anorak, he sees all this animation without really understanding it. A woman approaches him and reads him his own memories, recorded and saved by the Americans. ' I have been here since 1955. At first they wanted to make me leave. I did not want to go . . . ' A man could not show any greater emotion.

Claire Robinson is enthusiastic. 'What is great is to have found the architects who work freely on a project. For them, drawing the ZAC des Amandiers, the oldest urban renewal area in the capital, constitutes not only a case study but also a challenge to Paris.'

Sophie Cambazard, 'Americans Plan to Renovate the ZAC des Amandiers', Le Parisien, *Monday 22nd January 1995*

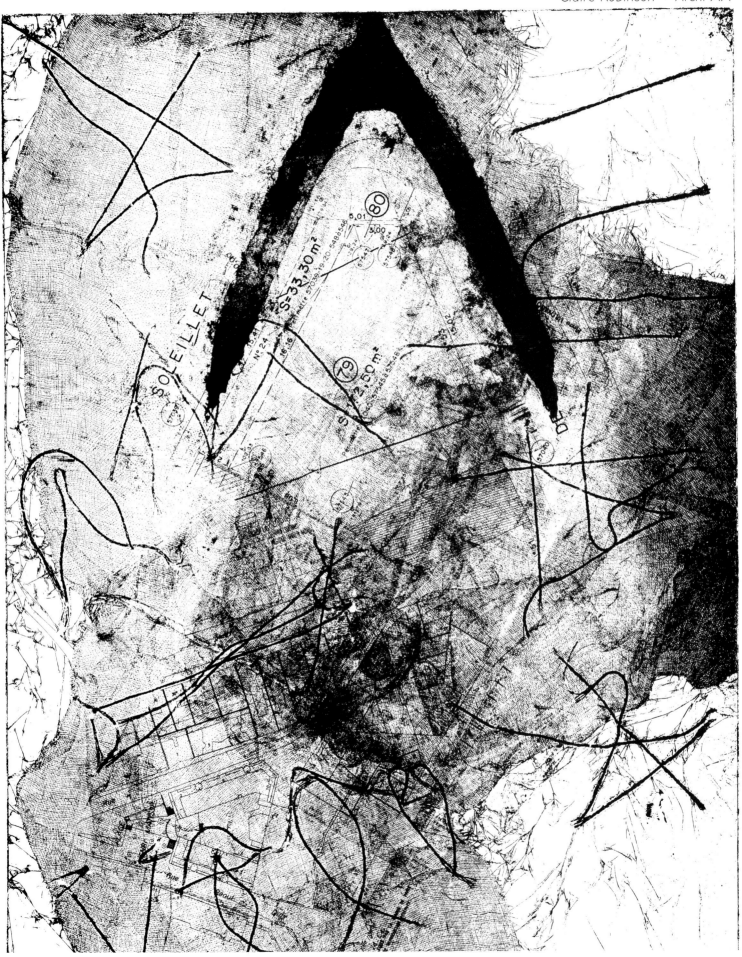

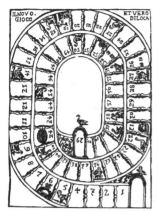

The Game of the Goose: invented in Italy where it was discovered by John Wolfe, a London printer, who claimed copyright on it in 1597. The Board is a spiral track with 63 numbered squares and five emblems: (1) the Bridge – a path; (2) the Well – a hole in space; (3) the Inn – a threshold; (4) the Prison – an enclosed space and (5) the Labyrinth – 1+2+3+4+5 closed and open simultaneously; the Goose Squares and the Dead Goose.

For Michel Serres, in *Language and Space: from Oedipus to Zola*, 1983, the Game of the Goose is a cultural paradigm; the emblems are spatial operators, tools for construction, connection and non-connection, linking, tying, opening bridges, making paths and forming relays between radically different spaces.

Key words : excess . negotiation . put together . restore

HEADROOM AND FLOWERING GIRLHOOD

Signal Yellow 512 Strand Polyester Nautical Line String Beam snaked through I section roof rafters and corrugated metal deck (fasteners exposed) and braided knotted and bowed to same with poor unwanted then lost then found multiple variety cotton bags and bag cotton remnants. Hoisted laced and strung every witch way by Mark mostly. And from the string beam also lashed to cantilever them where we want them hardwood bows and marionette style lathe (no unseen operator from above speaking dialogue) to hold the fishing line shining in threes to the centroid of each hoop – some hoola style – enamelled yellow, some Pocahontas fabric coated painted out orange, some natural banded PVC yellow off the rack, and some wreath style, bound grass wreath ready for holiday personalization in three sizes – fat wheat big wheat and *petite* wheat. These and others having been affixed to marionette style hardwood stays and bows by multiple forlorn ironed mostly by Hugh cotton bags or rags of bag cotton. Hoops then suspended at the other Mark's Adam's apple measure of the man to make the headroom horizon. Grown-up heads thereby severed with plenty of child's room in the body space below. Each hoop in its own fashion then worked upon with forlorn cotton bags and bag cotton baby pink tool champagne chiffon plain brown cotton twine white nylon parachute droppings etc in – among others – the schoolyard technologies of braiding lanyard style knotting rope jumping assorted tieings splicings scissorings slip knottings paper chaining and bow tyings not to mention attachments by some 14 gross shiny stainless steel dry cleaning safety pins. Each hoop named from the heart as follows: 10 Mama Dollies, Safety-Pin Harlequin, Double-Lobed Bee Sting, Chiffon Scorpion, Stripper with red socks, Stripper with yellow pockets, PL's Tails, Stringy Bangs, Curled Bob, Stripper with handbags, Baggy Weave, Snowflake, Paper Doll, Barely There Bags Under Your Eyes, Braided Braids then Braided, Knot Slipped and Snipped, Head In Curlers, Curvy Hairy Choker, Neat Pinked Pleats, Lacy Lantern, Flouncy Fat Bow, Spicy Spit Curl, Sissy Stripper with Bags, Chained and Tangled, Swirly Swinger, Fancy Formal Stripper, Unshapely Shift with Safety-Pin Squares, Eighty nine thousand two hundred and eighty square inches – Point zero zero three four seven two hoops per square inch – Nine million nine hundred forty thousand and seven hundred and sixty cubic inches above headroom horizon – Five million three hundred fifty six thousand and eight hundred cubic inches below headroom horizon.

Key words : excess . mere . space . word play

HEAVY NESS

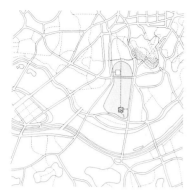

Demolition: At 3pm on 20th November 1994, the foreigner's apartments on Mount Namsan, Seoul, Korea were bombed – not by terrorists or subversives but under orders from the Government to restore the original profile of the sacred mountain. The Yongsan-gu district, until recently a US military golf course, was re-established as an open recreation area in 1991. This park will be the setting for the new National Museum of Korea. The aim of the Korean Ministry of Culture and Sports is that this museum will 'throw light on Korean history and culture in the context of the cultures of the whole world'.

A major road extension will reshape the eastern boundary of the Yongsan Family Park and provide an opportunity to suggest that the entire central park area could be given a new profile and internal organisation, releasing new potentialities. Our policy for the landscape and the building is the redescription and transformation of this existing situation, drawing out and discovering the potential in what is already there . . .

Finding edges: We have used a method which identifies the nearest smooth curved line that will join all the existing boundary conditions. This approach is applied to the edges of existing building and land forms at a variety of scales; at the scale of the region between the Korean War Memorial Museum and the proposed National Museum, and the locality of the proposed museum itself. Overlaps are found between different territories, and the potential of these overlaps developed.

Scribbling: Information on the location of existing surfaces is used to loosely determine the extent and overlap of local fields. The existing irregular edges of these fields are simultaneously smoothed and blurred by working repetitively over the same ground, sys-

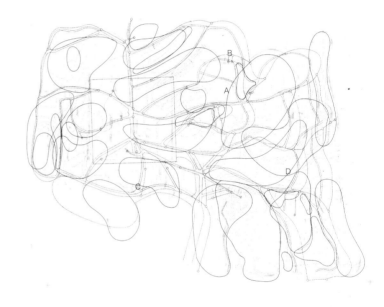

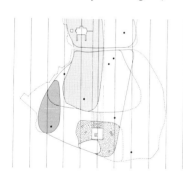

tematically scribbling, filling in the *blank* spaces (of the site/drawing) until there is nothing left. Repetitive tracing over the contours, pathways and streams reveals a web, pressure points and pressure zones and the conduits that connect them. Areas of overlap are categorised as zones of maximum intensity. Strange 3-dimensional concentrations emerge as the surface of the site appears to have become liquid.

Probes: These suggest locations for different kinds of intensive event spaces. Patterns are found in the overlapping, traces that can be coded according to specific material and organisational criteria. Some are enclosed but can be entered, some are closed, others open. Points of maximum intensity (entry points into the network) are chosen as the location for interactive information sites.

Plants: Existing planting is intensified by working within the pressure zones, discovering the surreal in the real – revealing strange and intriguing qualities in pre-existing arrangements.

Pools: Existing water bodies are enlarged to manipulate the spatial qualities of the park through reflection and ambiguities of distance.

ABOVE: +/- 3pm, 20th November 1994. New city datum emerging and cloud of 'foreign' particles
CENTRE: Finding edges: filled landscape – Yongsan Family Park re-described/scribbled
BELOW: Probes A.B.C.D.

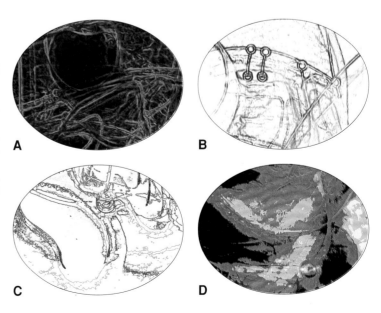

A **B**

C **D**

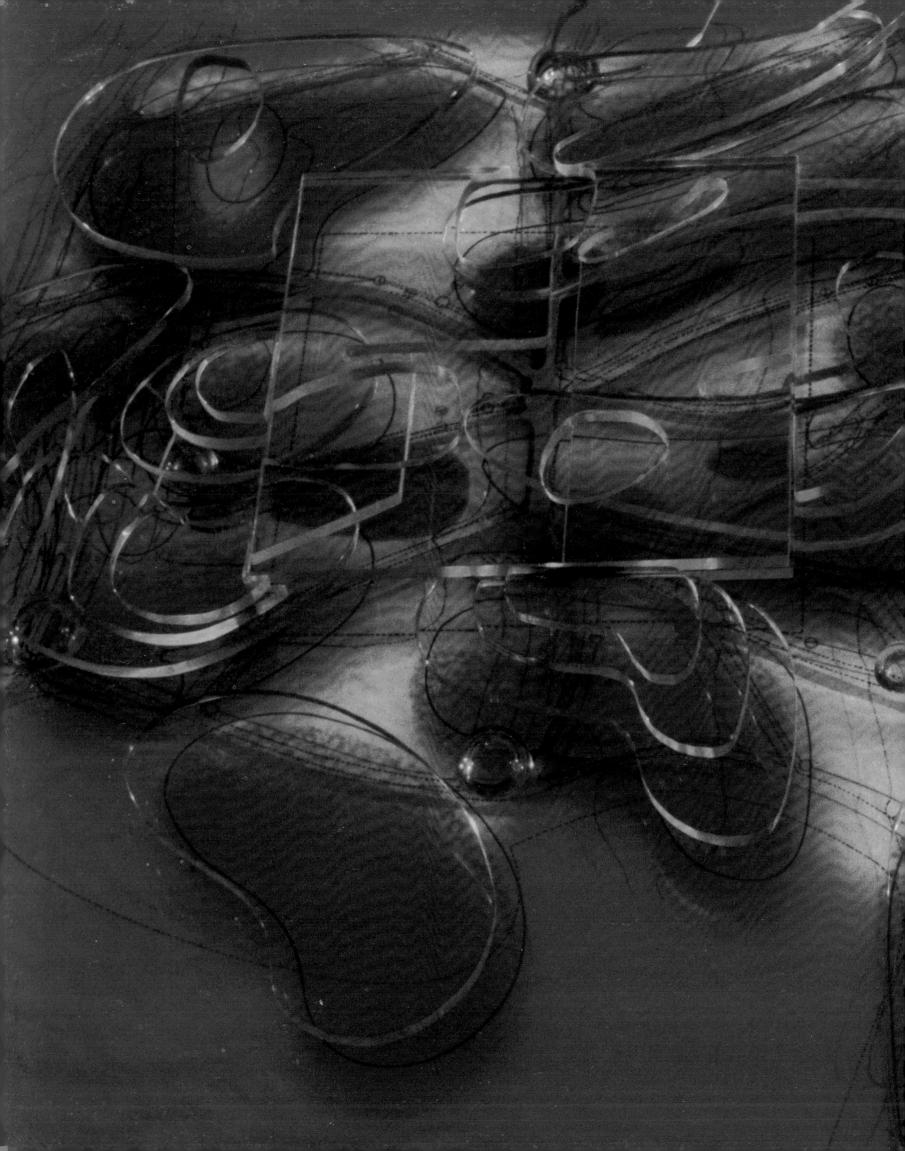

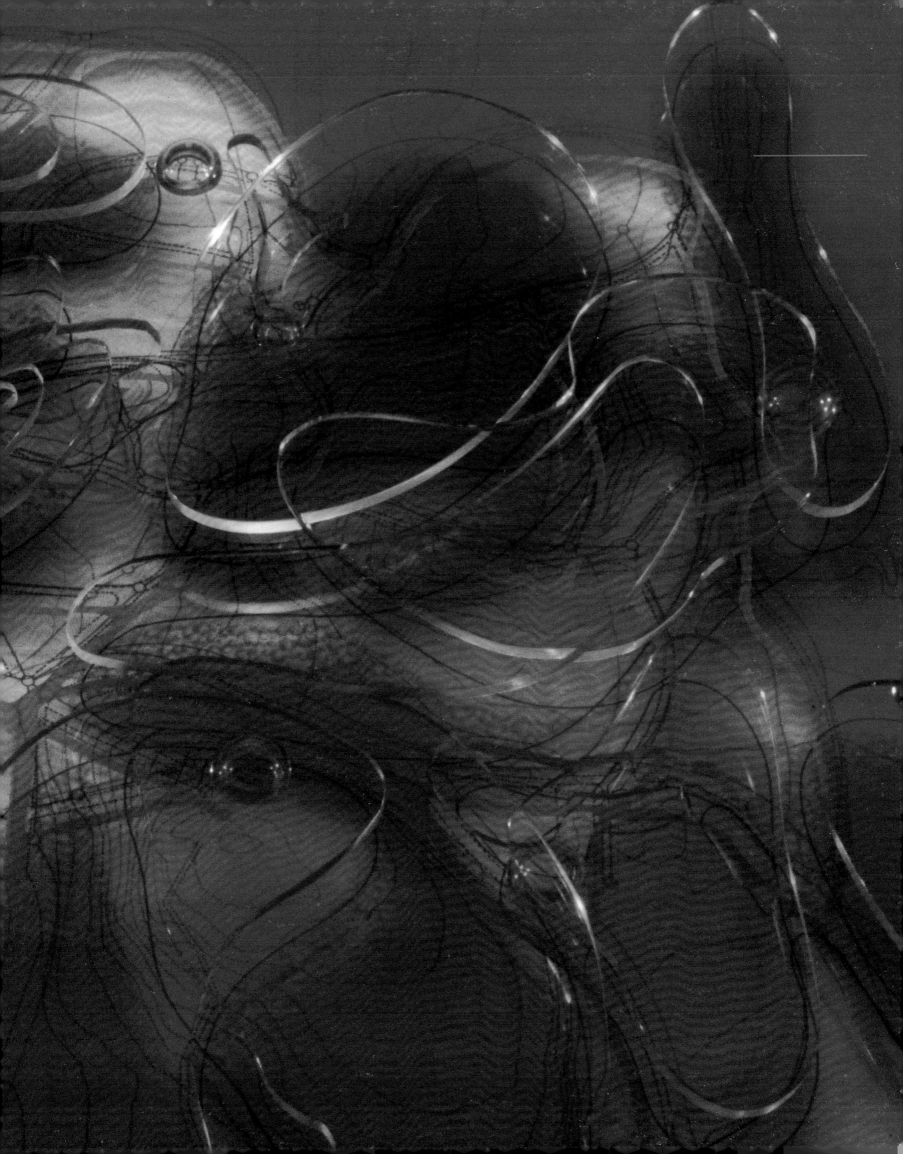

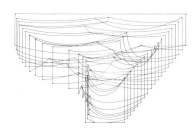

Dataspace: A museum is no longer a place purely for study or education. It is a place for entertainment and for learning-through-entertainment. A museum is also a venue for conventions, receptions and conferences of global, regional, national, corporate or local character. A museum is a place for the conservation of artefacts and a place for research which allows 'histories' to be constructed. It is a workshop, a warehouse, a studio, a school, a laboratory, a library, a theatre and a fairground, as well as a place of display.

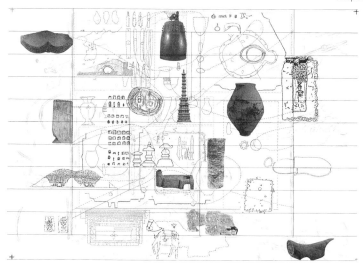

Acknowledging the hybrid character of the museum the structure is divided in two; a layer of mobile information (museum), over a layer of stable information (archive).

These are deformed and interconnected by:

[1] **interference** from the overlapping field conditions of the park, the *materialised* digressive web, and

[2] the impact of **weight**, local condensation.

The dataspace related to the exhibition and archival surfaces is compressed by three heavy objects: an auditorium, studios and a library/archive for text, enclosed concentrations of information which are specific, dense and 'blind'. These press down on the information space of the museum, *squeezing* the data, like the 3-dimensional objects passing through EA Abbot's *Flatland*, making physical (materialising) the otherwise *horizontal* space of data; a spatial condensation or compression, paradoxically suggesting the redistribution of information within the museum offering multiple readings, mixing aesthetic and historical values, redirecting and personalising the official, linear, hierarchical reading of Korean History .

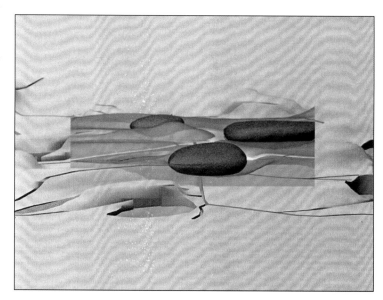

Reminder: The bombing of the foreigner's apartments is remembered/re-mind-ed by installing a permanent *'light' cloud* around Mount Namsan. This light object is the counterpart of the three *heavy objects* which deform the dataspace of the museum. The project proposes a non-physical but nevertheless palpable connection between the reflected light on the water of the River Han, the extreme materiality of the heavy objects (local compressions of data), the pressure zones and meridians in the park, the 'cloud' and the 'sacred' mountain.

[Credits: Jane Harrison, David Turnbull + Luis Castillo, Jung Hyung Hwang, Craig Kim, Daniel Lopez-Perez, David Phillips, Jonathan Weatherill, Gareth Wilkins; model – Aurorisa Mateo Rodriguez; computer images – Yasuhiro Santo]

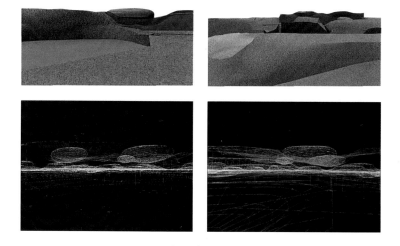

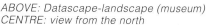

ABOVE: Datascape-landscape (museum)
CENTRE: view from the north
BELOW: 1 & 2 – the new Yongsan Family Park,
3 & 4 – Dataspace, mobile information with local condensations

Key words : accumulate . datascape . field . reincorporate . weight

HYPERTEXTUAL PICTURESQUE

Jennifer Bloomer

To turn to the landscape, or the garden, when thinking about architecture is to make a significant and difficult turn. The landscape in modernity has been figured as either supplemental or an accessorizing feature to the design of the building. To look at the potential of this architectural accessory requires an about-turn on the line of progress to look at the past, and to contemplate the riches of what came before the century of progress, that is the two that – now that we have made our turn – are receding down the line towards the vanishing point in much the same way that the future does when we peek back over our shoulders. In the webby historical-cultural panoply that comes to rest at points upon this line, we can see a number of 'accessories before the fact' of modernism, including the 18th-century English landscape garden tradition, with its stunning – visually affirming – relationship with the landscape painting tradition, and the writings of John Ruskin, the fellow who, in the 19th-century, was one of those guys who wrote a lot about the interesting relationships he perceived between architecture and culture, but built little. If, in our slight near-sightedness, we look at Ruskin's bulging pod (reticule?) of work way down the line, we see perhaps a quaint, but intriguing and historically important, supplement to 19th-century architecture in all its proper natural materiality and ornamentation all set to make a pretty architectural picture redolent of the kitschiest nostalgia. But, if we look with our handy two-way telescopes, zooming in, getting our noses right on the matter of the reading material, we can see something quite different, something that, for me, is astonishing.

At the place on the line where Le Corbusier's and Walter Gropius' great-grandmothers and grandfathers are children at play in the garden (1837), a series of articles called 'Villa and Cottage Architecture' appeared in *Loudon's Magazine of Architecture*. Here are a few excerpts.

> (W)hiteness destroys a great deal of venerable character, and harmonises ill with the melancholy tones of surrounding landscape: and this requires detailed consideration. Paleness of colour destroys the majesty of a building; first, by hinting at a disguised and humble material; and secondly, by taking away all appearance of age.

But, further on, following a note that the appearance of age in a villa is neither desirable nor necessary:

> We find, therefore, that white is not to be blamed in the villa for destroying its antiquity; neither is it reprehensible, as harmonising ill with the surrounding landscape; on the contrary, it adds to its brilliancy, without taking away from its depth of tone.
>
> If the colour is to be white, we can have no ornament, for the shadows would make it far too conspicuous, and we should get only tawdriness.[1]

These seemingly prescient words, so marvellously ornamented with the language of taste, were written by an 18-year-old boy named John Ruskin, who, engaged in the literary game of the *nom de plume*, wrote under the signature of one Kata Phusin. Aha, you may be thinking, everybody knows about Ruskin and his psycho-sexual problems: the frustrated love affair at 17 which 'seems to have been the effective cause of a permanent failure to attain emotional maturity'; the fact that his mother rented a cottage to be near him when he went to Oxford; his unwillingness to consummate his marriage, and about his ardent love at age 40 for a ten-year-old girl. A child who never grew up, one messed-up dude, is it any wonder the boy assumed that girlish name to mark his fledgling authorship? But look again. While Kata may carry a feminine connotation in its resemblance to Kate, *kata* is also the Greek word for 'according to' and *phusin* is, of course, the word for 'nature', from which comes the English word 'physics'. Kata Phusin – 'according to nature' – an early example of Ruskin's lifelong word play, is a rather authoritative persona indeed. Here is Mother Nature writing on the relation of domestic architecture, materiality, ornamental detail and colour in a manner that seems

to make an impetuous leap from the grass hut to the white villa (where colour and form override materiality). And whether we see this author as *Mater Natura* or John Ruskin, s/he seems an unlikely source for the fathers of the white box who will come along three generations later.

But let me tell you right now that a relation of causality between Ruskin and high modernism is not what I am after here. That is not my game. I am interested in something fleshier than such a simple line as that. Let me emphasize that although here Ruskin speaks to modernism, I do not suggest that, for example, Walter Gropius or Le Corbusier had read the essays in *Loudon's*. I am making a suggestion, instead, of the possibility of looking at the past in a different way, in a way perhaps similar to the way that we look at the future: as a mineable field for inspired invention.

In Kata Phusin's discourse, the building is not a 'machine in the garden', but a supplemental element of the landscape construed as a picture; a picture composed of hundreds of tiny details, in the mind of the taste making author/viewer. These articles form the germ of John Ruskin's 1842 paean to JMW Turner, the landscape painter, which praised for his 'truthful' depiction of nature in all its proliferation of colour and detail.

With these thoughts of architectural theory – the garden, landscape, proliferation, detail and mutating material – that our accessories before the fact give rise to, let us turn, or rather return, to that accessory after the fact, the computer, and what it gives rise to: electronic space. This is again a precipitous, however simple, turn, requiring us to move 180° once more on our little pivot point and look at a teeny piece of the intricate panoply that now faces us, the tiny little piece that is connected to the construction of these words I speak. We will call this piece 'The Hypertextual Picturesque', and Kata Phusin will introduce it:

> That which we foolishly call vastness is, rightly considered, not more wonderful, not more impressive, than that which we insolently call littleness.[2]

The Hypertextual Picturesque rests on the logic of the garden – the commingling of so many gendered games – exercised within electronic space. The materiality of electronic space is electronic image, where form and matter have a direct relation; both are reductive versions of our conventional notions of form and matter, a situation that offers the possibility of architectures that, because obeisant to convention, escape it. In this space, the figures one and nought are the codes that stand in simply for a duality of electronic impulse. In this space, representation and materiality share a direct, virtually unmediated relationship; they are nearly identical.

In the space of information, what is old and past – all the facts, images and documents of history – merges fluidly with what is new and now – all the information, images and electronic documents. In the space of information, there is a seamlessness of time and space which mirrors – reversed perhaps – the intensity of seamless time and space that characterizes modernism.

The relationships of landscape, architecture, painting, the interweave of time and space, old and new, and constructions assembled from plethora upon plethora of detail, define the old and much maligned concept of the Picturesque. The Picturesque, a collection of aesthetic theories and ideas that addressed the way we look at and make landscapes, was a phenomenon of the late 18th and early 19th centuries. Because I do not have the time to digress into a discussion of it, I will simply list here some characteristics of the Picturesque:

• An emphasis on detail over overall form.
• An emphasis on image; the manipulation of the three-dimensional so that it conforms to a two-dimensional image.
• The controlled use of the distant; geography and chronology.
• The use of the found object, passive matter; glorification of the ugly and ordinary.
• A foregrounding of matter and its physical phenomena, ie, 'nature'.

Jennifer Bloomer

- A challenge to the idea of private property.
- An emphasis on variety and idiosyncrasy.
- The object of the tourist as a collector of pictures of places.

The Picturesque is situated between the aesthetic characteristics of the beautiful and the sublime, but unlike either it appeals only to one sense: vision.

Perhaps I do not need to mention that all of these characteristics of the Picturesque also are descriptive of the phenomenon of cyberspace. Listen as I read the words of William Gilpin, written in 1794:

The first source of amusement to the picturesque traveller, is the pursuit of his object – the expectation of new scenes continually opening, and arising to his view. We suppose the country to have been unexplored. Under this circumstance the mind is kept constantly in an agreeable suspense. The love of novelty is the foundation of this pleasure. Every distant horizon promises something new; and with this pleasing expectation we follow nature through all her walks. We pursue her from hill to dale; and hunt after those various beauties with which she everywhere abounds.[3]

The condition of electronic space may also be described by these words of Raimonda Modiano on the Picturesque:

... the Picturesque desire remains free and unattached, continuously disconnecting from specific objects in order to return to the self or move on to another object.[4]

Furthermore:

When desire is thus barred from its object, vision itself becomes appetite. I would like to suggest that the Picturesque traffics heavily in the erotics of denied desire, relegating appetite to the exclusive realm of vision which at once limits and sustains it. The Picturesque abounds in 'wistful gazes toward untouchable objects', and features perpetual brides and bridegrooms who never consummate their 'affair with the landscape' . . .[5]

Do you hear the succinct alignment of the space of the Picturesque with the space of the computer, glued together by the metaphor of the land as an object of sexual desire? But this landscape object, unlike that of Sir Walter Raleigh and others, is untouchable. Untouchable because its materiality and its desirability exist through infinite numbers of images.

To theorize a new game played on old ground, by theorizing an old game played in new space, is logically appropriate within the necessary reflexivity of such a game. The constant pivoting and shuttling between old and new, big and small, with its concomitant confusion of good and bad, masculine and feminine etc, is the mechanism of the garden and the landscape. It is also the mechanism that structures this paper. The garden as I have used it is a metaphor of effect and event, not of formal causality. Everything is potentially on the move, coming and going, repeating patterns, but the effect of the repetition is always a little or a lot different. This construction, like the garden, is a phenomenon of

cyclic consumption and a production of its own materiality.

The Hypertextual Picturesque is an architecture of flickering texts and images. It is an aggregation of detail. It is a spatial construction within the computer which does not mine conventional architectural notions of space, or of representation, but which does mine conventional architectural notions of construction. The materiality of the computer is its materiality; the Hypertextual Picturesque cannot therefore be reproduced in three-dimensions, although it bears the potential to provide generative, methodological impetus to three-dimensional construction. Furthermore, it is a notion that circumscribes a reconsidered relation of city and garden. The Hypertextual Picturesque could not be classified as hyperspace, but it is constructed within the hyperspatial. It is a flickering hybrid (now you see it, now you don't) of something old and something new, the infinitely large and the infinitely small.

The picturesque landscape and the picturesque tour exist in reference to the idea of home. No matter how far one ventures into the geographical or chronological distance, there is at every point or moment the possibility of a loop in the itinerary that returns to the starting point. This home base, this safe domestic space, is an implicit, but necessary, condition of the picturesque tour that parallels that of the cyberventurer, who can always loop back to SHUT DOWN. The garden play of my children, the games of any children, are also played in reference to home in its material, formal and metaphorical possibilities. When the games stop, children, sometimes eagerly, sometimes reluctantly, return home, whether it be grass hut, white stucco villa or the arms of a sheltering parent.

And now, this little game can stop for awhile. You know where to go.

Hypertext: tries to reproduce the workings of the mind, the brain's associative references. A Hypertext is open-ended, a narrative whose structure, logic and closure fluctuate. Hypertext mimics the non-linear aspects of human thought; it also shapes the mental worlds and problem solving skills of the individual user. Hypertext influences the way that we think. The sense of fragmentation is compensated by the connectivity – the possibility of establishing multiple links between different spaces.

Notes

1 Kata Phusin, *The Poetry of Architecture: Cottage, Villa, etc*, John Wiley, (New York) 1837, p 222.
2 Ibid. p66.
3 William Gilpin, 'On Picturesque Travel', *Three Essays: On Picturesque Beauty; On Picturesque Travel; and On Sketching Landscape: To Which is Added a Poem, On Landscape Painting*, (London) 1794, pp47-48.
4 Raimonda Modiano, 'The legacy of the Picturesque', *The Politics of the Picturesque*, ed. Stephen Copely and Peter Garside, Cambridge University Press, (Cambridge) 1994, p214, n3.
5 Ibid. p197.

Key words : hypertext

INTERRUPTIONS

Robert Lawson

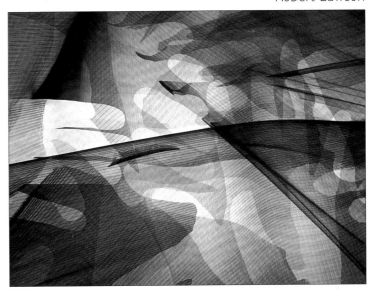

Interruptions is the title of an ongoing series of 'objectless' and 'cameraless' photographs, which explores the patterning effects of spatial and temporal interruptions of a light beam. The most functional of interruptions, that of the light by photosensitive paper, results in exposure. The procedure is a kind of light drawing where the paper moves and the light beam remains static. Image variations are produced by changing the speed and pattern of the motion, curving the plane of the paper, incorporating a light-blocking object or developing the image, re-exposing and redeveloping in chromogenic developer. Other variations come from interruptions, such as knocking the paper causing the axis of rotation to change, improvising pauses and rate variations in the rotation or manually blocking or unblocking the beam at random intervals.

This series illustrates variations which occur when patterns evolving from preset, relentless, mechanical parameters are 'interrupted' by random, improvised human gestures.

Key words : hesitation . space . spectre

KLAPPER HALL

Vito Acconci

The site is a plaza in front of the English department building on a college campus. A stairway leads up to the building; on either side of the stairway a pedestal holds a granite sphere 92cm in diameter.

The programme is an activated plaza.

The proposal is that the existent spheres are not left alone; the existent spheres are mixed into a world of spheres.

The plaza, in front of the building, becomes a field of bouncing balls; the existent spheres have their place in a range of spheres, from 46-320cm in diameter.

The spheres are usable: a sphere is cut in two to make a passage through it . . . a niche is cut into a sphere to form a seat . . . a niche is cut around a sphere to provide group seating . . .

The spheres provide lighting for the plaza; light comes from within the spheres, from behind the cuts in the spheres.

The spheres run wild: one climbs a stairway . . . one is about to roll down (or up) a ramp . . . one has gotten to the top of the building . . .

[Queen's College, New York, 1993-1995. Credits: Acconci Studio, Luis Vera; Design & Engineering – Won Chang, Robert Bedner; Contractor – Peter Homestead; Fabricator – MB Winston.]

Key words : field . play . re-creation . wildlife

LANGUAGE-GAMES

Alison Mark

Words, the wall material of the symbolic order, are as likely to break our bones (our matrix) as are sticks and stones.
Jennifer Bloomer

In the beginning was the word: language is the most powerful of games, not because of what it can itself do, but because of what it can cause to be done, what it constructs. Despite this, however material we understand language to be, it is not 'the wall material of the symbolic order' which breaks our bones, but the operations of the human context in which the language is used. The wisdom of Wittgenstein's formulation of the language-game lies precisely in this recognition. 'I shall call the whole, consisting of language and the actions into which it is woven, the 'language-game'. That is, this game – whose name is legion – does not consist of language alone, but also the context of human behaviour in which the lexical items occur. Without this (and not infrequently with it) it would often be difficult, if not impossible, to interpret what is being said. Since communication is the primary aim of language, it may inevitably be what Wittgenstein called 'the language of information', but it is not always, as he observed in the case of that particular organisation of language called a poem, 'the language-game of giving information'. And it is precisely in this capacity to move lexical items – and the reader/writer – from one language-game to another that the generative, or more properly, transformative power of playing games with language lies. For they bring with them to the new context the ghost of the other, its resonances transmutating in the field of the new.

In *The Oxford A-Z of Word Games* there are over 250 listed games, all of which rely for their operation on playing with the connections between different words (chain of signifiers), between words and their conceptual meaning (signifieds) or the connections between words and objects in the world (reference). That is, they rely upon systems of rules which they rarely articulate, but through which they achieve their significance by either conformity or deviation. (Change the rules and you change the language-game.) Attempts to get outside this circulatory system of language and its production have proven so problematic that an 'outside' to language can hardly be envisioned: how can we articulate such an idea, but with language? But for all the notorious slipperiness of words, there has to be some area of agreement or no communication is possible. Creativity in language, productivity in language, lies in the capacity of the speaker or writer to transform units which are recognisable in themselves by changing the context in which they are employed. Change the rules and you change the language-game, and you change the meaning, without changing what is being said: irony provides a prime example, as do those thoroughly post-modern techniques of parody and pastiche. Pleasure in language – sensuous as much as cognitive – and problems of communication have this same source; pleasure and pain.

Being born into language, as with all births, involves a separation: a split, to which we are introduced by the first, the natal cut. And any split involves a loss, however infinitesimal. The split is mimed linguistically in marks like parentheses, obliques, hyphens, which at once imply relations and subvert them. These marks are not themselves words, but they change our relationships to the words (the context) in which they occur. They can indicate provisionality, doubt, or subordination, and simultaneously draw attention to a split and an attempt to bridge it. And so we can begin to subvert the pretensions of the symbolic order to deny loss: to substitute its virtuality for that reality. Hence, the disaffection of melancholia (preservation) displaces the possibility of mourning (acknowledgement of loss) and the potentiality of the new. The language-games provides a possible strategy with which to outmanoeuvre the melancholia of saturated language.

Key words : word play

LES HALLES FAÇADE

Paul Edwards/Ou. Pho. Po.

Factual description: the mirror covered building is the corner of Les Halles in Paris, facing the intersection of the rue Pierre Lescot and the rue Rambuteau. *Les Halles, Façade* was made out of an ordinary black and white photograph enlarged onto a 26 x 21cm glossy resin-coated paper. The procedure for conversion to 3 - Dimensions is as follows:
(1) Cut-out the sky
(2) Score, using a ruler and compass point or blade, on the front for folds intended to fold backwards.
(3) Score on the back for folds that are to be pinched forwards.
The base of the photograph must not be a straight line if the facade is to stand up.

The cut-out, scored and folded stand-up photograph can be folded flat, faxed and rebuilt without instructions.

Key words : play . make-believe . un-forget

LEWIS HOUSE

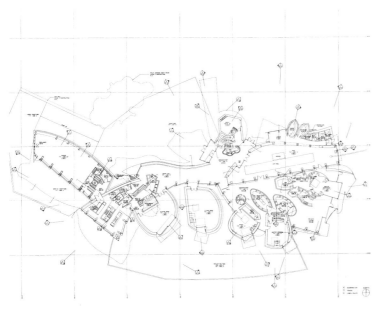

The result of a collaborative exploration of forms and ideas between Frank O Gehry as lead design architect, Philip Johnson as collaborating design architect and artists Richard Serra, Larry Bell, Claes Oldenburg and Coosje Van Bruggen and the late Maggie Keswick. A 2044m² house for Peter B Lewis located in nine acres of woodland on a hilltop in Lyndhurst, Ohio, a suburb of Cleveland.

This complex accumulation of forms and flows was developed initially as a physical model, and then digitized so that it could be drawn – moving back and forth between manual and virtual manipulation, ceaselessly. Representing another form of collaboration; cyborg intelligence.

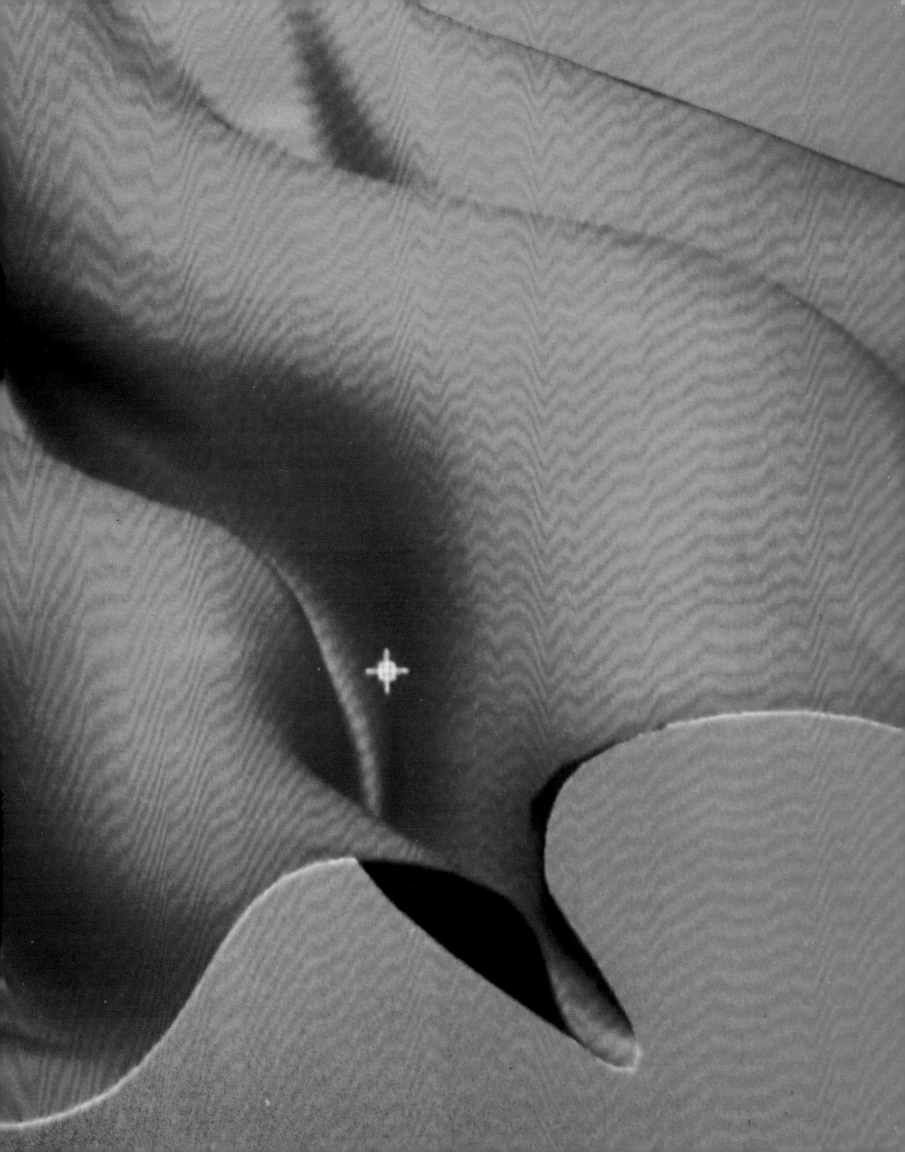

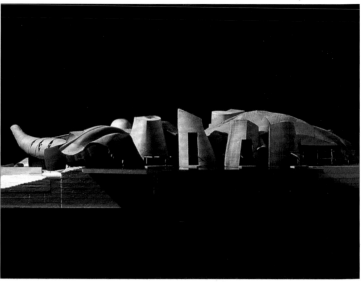

Organizationally the house negotiates spatial continuity and discontinuity installing room/objects – 'whatever critters were lying around' – both in and around a polymorphous sequence of rooms; amorphous objects that are paradoxically both inside the inside and outside the outside.

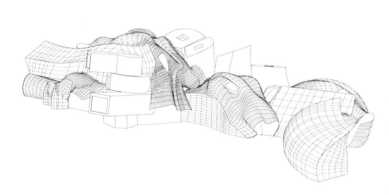

Comprised of the Four Sentinels – The Fish in the Garage, Viking Ship(s), The Octopus (by Philip Johnson) and A Prehistoric Horse/ Snake(s). The interior residual space is the most highly charged and differentiated.

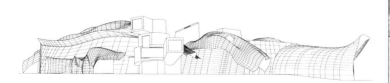

The form of the draped velvet surface – hardened using wax in the physical model – distilled several forms including a horse's head; animistic recognition.
Key words : gaming . negotiation . re-call . written

LIGHT NESS

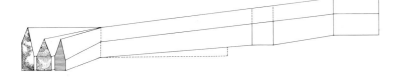

Exploration: Literal transparency – 'Material' (see below). Programmatic transparency – example: work (factory) through display (museum) through education (university), all combinations possible, all variable.

Technique: Un-focussed relations, random generation of pathways, scatter, regression, cross-referencing of use, categories, randomly generated formal disfigurations.

Material: Glass-fritted; stained; coloured; translucent (variable); mirrored (variable); opaque (too many combinations: bottles bulbs vases vitrines mirrors windows lights glasses doors televisions bowls lenses cases screens boxes jugs swords windscreens test-tubes phials pipettes beakers slippers jars frames . . .), reflected, refracted, distorted.

Envelope: Adopts the constructional methods of nondescript, inexpensive factory or sales buildings which can be found everywhere; regards these as exemplary; follows the shape of the site literally; adopts and combines recognizable forms of industrial and heritage buildings; manipulates the recognizable to be both familiar and strange, anamorphic distortion; a single skin with articulated ends.

Image: Commonplace images (any/various) folded over the envelope, enlarged or reduced (too many pixels) – never and yet paradoxically always recognizable.

Information: Camera + monitor field; excessive surveillance (too many points of view), with randomized relay/playback sequence combining production, exhibition and education information sampled from sites within the envelope/building (interaction points – sites of maximum compression/crossover), and random signals from outside (local, cable and global television and Internet): superabundance as catharsis.

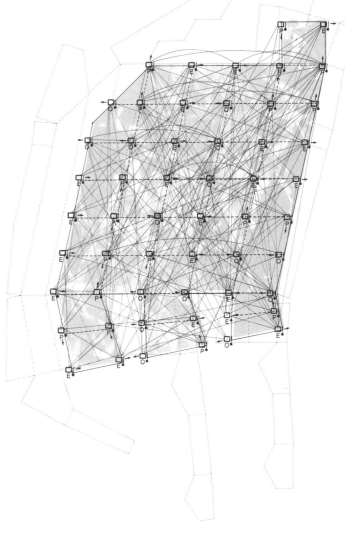

Composite image: programmatic field + fold + profile + information field

P = production
O = observation
E = education

[National Glass Centre, Sunderland: Jane Harrison, David Turnbull + Craig Kim, Won Kyung Paik]

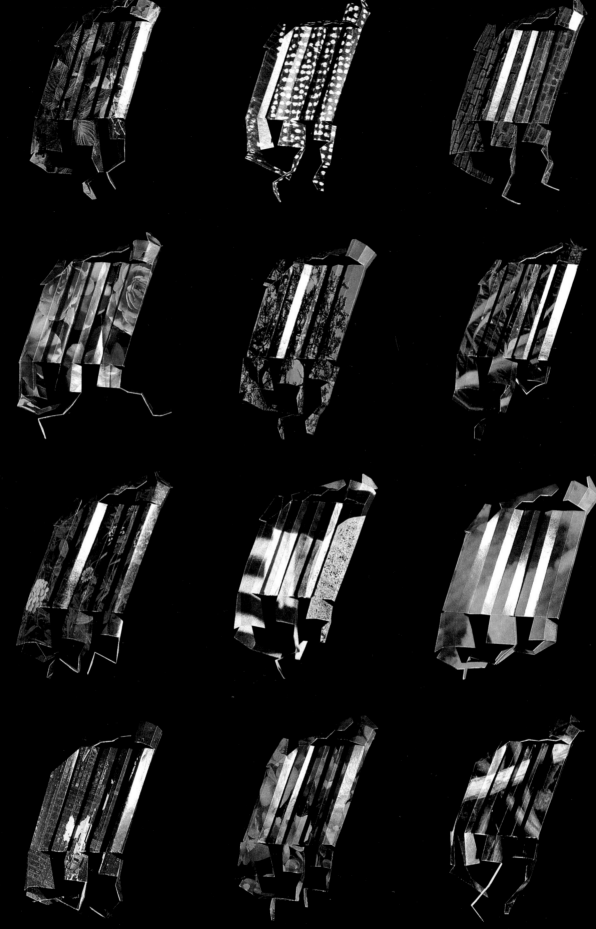

Key words : distortion . landscape . random . superficial

MERE . . .

Liquid Inc

Mere   Mere is not pejorative. It means famous, glorious, and beautiful.

La Mère   Mother in French. Not father. Not master.

Sea   *La Mer* also the sea.. The sea has waves. The sea is Liquid. The sea fluctuates and seeps. A liquid see.

[*Column Corset, Building Bustle* (detail), 1994: millinery foam, hex net, brushed aluminium stays, African-American synthetic hair, lead fishing weights, stainless steel knots with wings.]

Key words : flow . ghost . inconsequential

MICRO-MACRO

Jae-Eun Choi

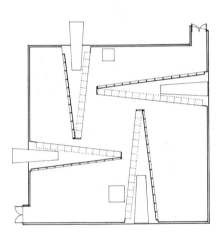

Micro-Macro is composed of two spaces located within the Japanese Venice Biennale Pavilion; the outer walls of the pavilion and the piloti (underground). Within the piloti, large-scale transparencies (static) and videos (animated) of microbes are installed. The microbes, cultivated from the buried papers, are magnified 20,000-50,000 times. The space created is maze-like and disorienting. Here, the self-organizing characteristics of ecosystems, and the continuous character of the space are central themes.

The outer walls of the pavilion are covered with multicoloured plastic piping. The material was selected paradoxically for its beauty, translucency and convenience and for the ecological problems caused by plastic's manufacture and disposal. The colours of the plastic pipes correspond to the colours used by Mongolian nomads, whilst the translucency of the plastic permits extraordinary effects to be produced by the light as it shines through the walls. Although the plastic pipes were straight at the opening of the exhibition, over time they have warped and changed their form.

The two installations, outer and inner, macro and micro, apparently have no connection. It is intended that by placing two things together without apparent resemblance, but linked environmentally and ecologically, a new structure is formed. Everything is controlled by 'Time'.

[outside walls: size – 16m x 9m x 4m; sides – 8 tons plastic pipe scaffolding system; installation area – 250 m²; medium – acrylic sheets, transparency, television monitors, LD, neon light.]

Key words : continuous charge . composition . ground . surface

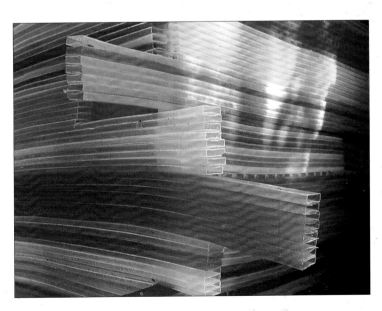

MICRO-MACRO

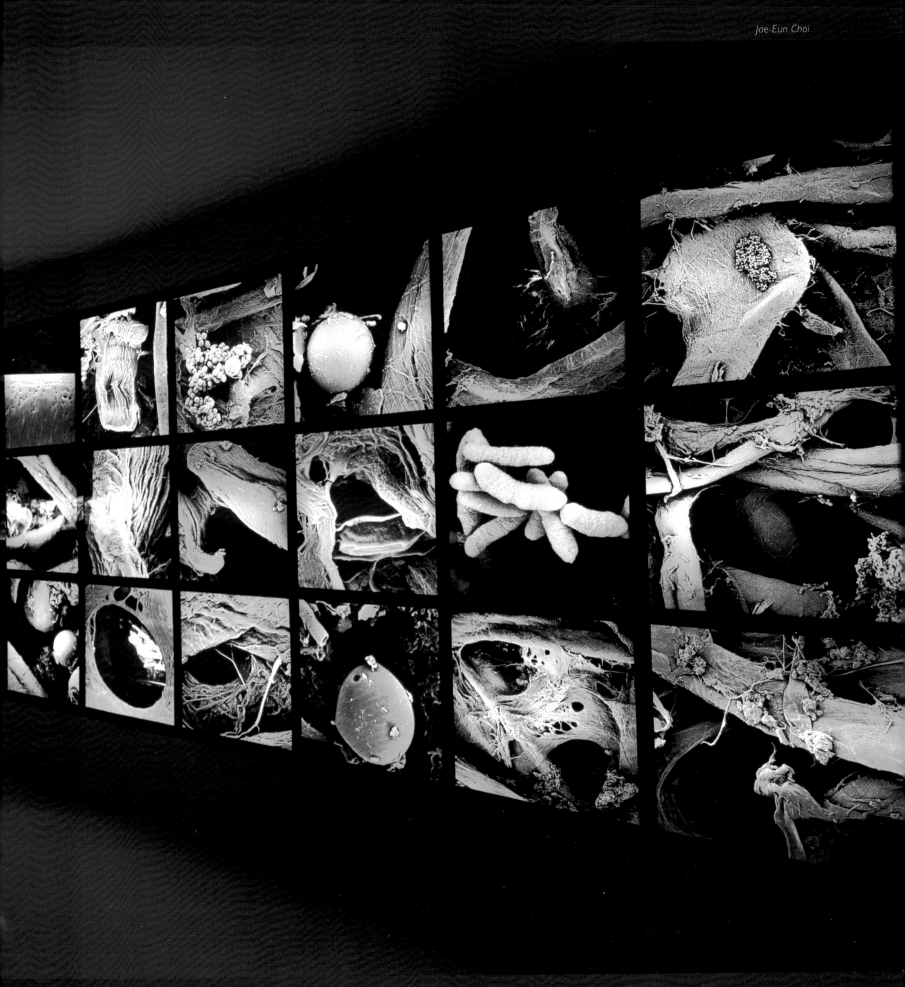

Jae-Eun Choi

MONUMENTAL PROPAGANDA

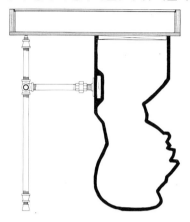

Mac Adams
Valeriy Aisenberg
Carl Andre
Vladimir Arhipov
Armand Arman
Olga Ast
Yuriy Avvakumou
Maria Baburova
Alexander Filipov
Vagrich Bakhchanyan
Sergei Bazilev
Robert Beckmann
Gary Beeber
Deborah Freeman
Zigi Ben-Haim
Dominique Blain
Farid Bogdalov
Constantin Boym
Alden carr
Génia chef
Igor Chelkovski
Olga Chernyshova
Petah Coyne
Irina Danilova
Orshi Drozdik
Vladimir Dubosarskiy
Ericson & Ziegler
Simon Faibisovich
John Fekner
Don Leicht
Vadim Fishkin
Judith Fleishman
Kurt Gebauer
Michel Gerard
Marina Temkina
Alex Grey
Judith Harvest
Stephen Hennessy
Susan Hoeltzel
Medgermeneutica

Irwin
Alesksy Isaev
Menashe Kadishman
Jim Kempner
Georgii Kiesewalter
Ilia Kitup
Shirley Klinghoffer
Komer & Melamid
Igor Kopystiansky
Svetlana Kopystiansky
Joseph Kosuth
Nina Kotel
Vladimir Salinkov
Marko Kovacic
Nicolai Kozlov
Eli Kuslansky
Leonid Lam
Thomas Lawson
Leighlane
Leonid Lerman
Les Levine
Georgii Litichevsky
Anton Litvin
Liz-N-Val
Julia Lorinczy
Igor Makarevich
Nieves Micas
Miralda
Roberto Mitrotti
Robert C Morgan
Igor Moukhin
John Murray
Irina Nakhova
Vladimir Nekrasov
Timur Novikov
Vladimir Paperny Ass
Peter Ohilips
Ilia Piganov
Nikolai Punin
Boris Ravvin

David Robbins
Michael Robertson
Andrei Roiter
Lolita Romanova
Gail Rothschild
Stephen Furnstahl
Christy Rupp
Yuri Rybchinsky
U Nikich
Aidan Salachov
Serge Samusenko
Joel sanders
Mark Tsurumaki
Barbara Santoro
Alexander Savko
Scherer & Ouporov
Buky Schwartz
Sintes
Alisa Snezina
Leonid Sokov
Andrew Solomon
Art Spiegelman
Vitutas Stasunas
Michelle Stuart
Andrew Szczepaniec
Jorge Tacla
Mark tansey
Marina Telepneva
Victor Tupitsyn
Liselot van der Heijden
Oleg Vassiliev
Sergeiy Volochov
Laurence Warshaw
Florence Weisz
Krzysztof Wodiczko
Nina Yankowitz
Maria Zazelyapina
Dimitry Likin
Olga Ziangirova
Alexander Zosimov

'Monumental Propaganda' (1993) is a travelling exhibition featuring more than 150 contemporary artists' proposals for the transformation and preservation of the former Soviet Union's obsolete totalitarian monuments. The exhibition design for 'Monumental Propaganda' – first installed in the Courtyard Gallery at the World Financial Centre from 22nd July to 3rd October 1993 – organizes a vast array of materials within a system of display that is also a visual and conceptual response to the exhibition theme.

The artists' proposals, all works on paper in various mediums, are presented horizontally in a series of 26 display cases designed specifically for the exhibition. Each case is made of unfinished plywood and supported by a plaster bust of Stalin; balanced on its head with an armature of black iron pipe and fittings. The cases are arranged in a gallery-long procession passing before a model of an artist's proposal for Lenin's Mausoleum, forming an ironic re-enactment of a May Day parade of armaments through Red Square. The walls of the gallery display no work but are painted a deep red, creating a huge banner for the exhibition, visible from the other sides of the courtyard.
[The exhibition was instigated by a call for proposals from the Russian-American artists Vitaly Komar and Alexander Melamid, and was organized and curated by Independent Curators Incorporated.]

Key words : accumulate . act-out . call-again . naming . re-member

MORPHOLO

Thieri Foulc/Ou. Pein. Po.

The MORPHOLO is a 'combinatoria' of square tiles (*carreaux*) which can be arranged in different manners, as a game, or as art. The tiles, which contain black and white shapes, can be juxtaposed at will, yielding (at least) several billion unforeseen larger shapes. There is only one rule: you must match, on the edges, black against black and white against white.

The generation of the material

Take a square (*carré*). Each side may be divided in half, and each half-side (or 'half-edge') may be designated black or white. For each side, there are four possible structures: white + white (all white), white + black, black + white, black + black (all black). For the square, with its 4 sides, there are therefore $4^4 = 256$ possible structures.

The tiles may be numbered according to the order of their generation:

n	1er côté	2e côté	3e côté	4e côté	n	1er côté	2e côté	3e côté	4e côté
1	W+W	W+W	W+W	W+W	7	W+W	W+W	W+B	B+W
2	W+W	W+W	W+W	W+B	8	W+W	W+W	W+B	B+B
3	W+W	W+W	W+W	B+W	17	W+W	W+B	W+W	W+W
4	W+W	W+W	W+W	B+B	65	W+B	W+W	W+W	W+W
5	W+W	W+W	W+B	W+W	193	B+B	W+W	W+W	W+W
6	W+W	W+W	W+B	W+B	256	B+B	B+B	B+B	B+B

If you orient the square according to the order of its sides, you get 256 different structures. However, if you then rotate it 90°, 180° or 270°, you discover superimposed structures. In total, 240 tiles are 'quadruplons' (fourfolded structures), capable of being superimposed 4 by 4; 12 tiles are 'doublons' (twofolded structures), capable of being superimposed 2 by 2; and 4 tiles are, might one say, 'unicons' (onefolded structures).

By applying the mathematical principle of 'reducing to an equation', it is possible to define an abridged MORPHOLO, which consists solely of $60+6+4 = 70$ tiles of totally different structure. The particular distribution of white and black along the edges of either the 256 or 70 squares constitutes an example of what may be called an 'edge constraint'.[1] This is a formal rule, comparable to the 'fixed forms' that are frequently observed in literature, but seldom in the plastic arts. The rule does not interfere with the working of the artist's imagination: the shapes on the surface of the squares can be varied freely. Nor does this rule guarantee a result: like the framework of the ballad or sonnet, it is 'capable' of bad or good. It all depends on: (1) the artist drawing the tiles: (2) the combinations that come into play.

Play applications

Once the tiles have been generated, the first reflex is to play with them, to combine them in the above manner while observing the 'edge rule': the juxtaposition of white and white, black and black. In practice, however, players supplement this basic rule with other rules.

a: The area of play. Do you choose an infinite field, or limit the area of play? If the latter, to what extent or form do you limit it? With a complete MORPHOLO consisting of 256 tiles – which we'll call pieces – you could limit play to a square with a side of $\sqrt{256} = 16$ pieces. Problem: would it be possible to fill such an area completely by following the rule of juxtaposition? How many solutions are there? At this time (1996), patient experimenters have already discovered two different solutions. Computers are on the spot . . . The colour of the play area, in any case, would have to be mid-grey (*gris moyen*), to give equal balance to white and black edges.

b: Distribution of pieces amongst the players. Do you divide up all the pieces straight away, or leave a reserve?

c: Opening move. One possibility is to let the player with the piece containing the smallest number of black half-edges begin the game.

d: Different rules of play. After a certain point players might have to add pieces that connect not just to one side, but to at least two.

Advantage could also be given to players who manage to place pieces which connect on three, or even four sides at a time. They might gain one, even two more turns, which would allow them to get rid of their pieces as quickly as possible.

e: The end-point of the game. The winner would be the first person to get rid of all their pieces.

However, as you can see, such an operation is purely formal, purely for the sake of play. It creates nothing, except winners and losers.

Artistic application

True artists would leave such competitiveness to others. Observing the same principles of juxtaposition, they would attempt instead to create beautiful, interesting forms. They would not so much play, as amuse themselves.

They would only place their piece – their tile – once they were sure they were making a felicitous addition to the overall picture – one contributing to the creation of a larger shape that would stimulate the other participants.

They would avoid points and closures, understand the alternation of abstract and figurative forms, and notice that not all the white shapes were 'blank', but that, on the contrary, some of them could be exploited as representational shapes on a black 'ground' (dialectic of figure ground).

They would not be in the least concerned about whose turn it was to play. As they would not be playing, they would not have a turn. They would listen to the advice of their partners and undo part of the work in progress as often as they would take pleasure in redoing another part in a different way.

Murals

It is possible to create a complete room – floor, walls and ceiling – by distributing 256 tiles in the following manner. Floor and ceiling squares consisting of 8x8 = 64 tiles. Four walls consisting of 8x4 = 32 tiles. Doors and windows, also tiles, based on the same module (and included in the count). One tile = 80cm per side. Complete room: 6.40m x 6.40m x 3.20m.

This potential application has been achieved using Diasec® squares which are backed with a film of Ferriflex® magnetised rubber. The magnetized squares are attached to a metallic armature, and they can be moved around at will. In this way the decor of the mural can be changed on daily basis.

Problem: how many ways are there of arranging the complete MORPHOLO on this parallelepipid area?

Other problems

• Order: Tiles can be arranged according to the order of their generation, from 1 to 256. But there are other methods. The beginner has first to invent methods of ordering.

• Study how many combinations are possible in relation to the form or extent of the area of play, ie, if the 256 tiles are displayed, not on a 256-square area, but on an area equal to 400 or 1024 squares for example.

• Describe the structure of a MORPHOLO in three colours, where the edge of each square is divided into 3. This would give $3^3 = 27$ solutions for each side, and thus $27^4 = 531441$ solutions for the square, and as many tiles for the complete MORPHOLO.

• Expound the general problem of an x-colour and y-edge MORPHOLO (the tiles of which being nevertheless able to be placed side by side on a plane; there are only 17 geometric figures known to satisy this requirement).

• Compile classification tables for pieces in different types of MORPHOLO. Describe the use of these tables for statistical, astrological, geodesic, divinatory purposes.

NOTES

1 Various species of edge constraints have been elaborated by the Ou. Pein. Po., such as Bitangential Picturogenesis, Carelman's Representational Dominoes, Aline Gagnaire's Polyptykon, etc.

Key words : algorithm . foreplay . negotiation

Thieri Foulc/Ou. Pein. Po.

Key words : make-believe . put together . repetition . rule-govern-play

(translated by Pamela Johnston)

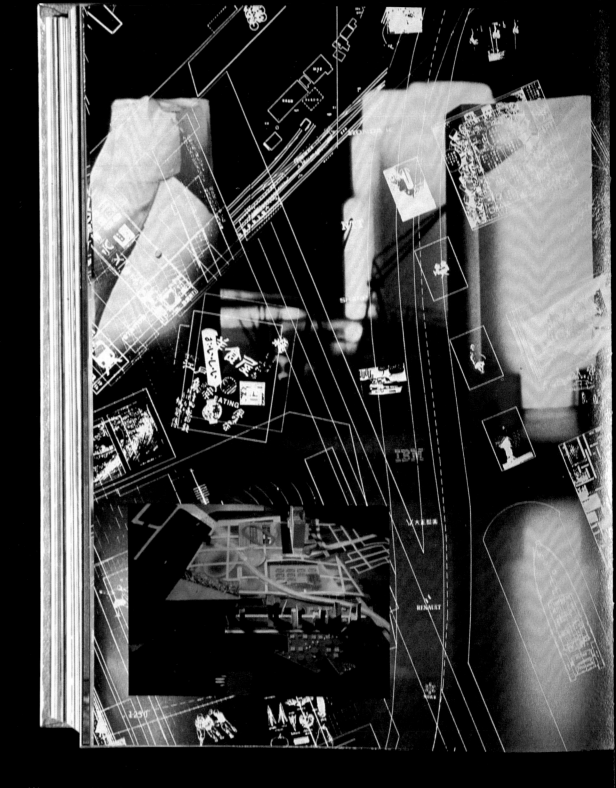

We went to Yokohama.

Yokohama is a port city south of Tokyo, and as in most port cities the harbour activity is pulling away toward the sea, leaving vast abandoned territories.

Along the perimeter of Yokohama's bay the city identified five sites that could be redeveloped to form a circle, five kilometres in diameter, that would be completed by a new bridge. They asked a group of architects and artists to imagine this circle.

Our site is next to a future city – Minato Mirai 21 – which in 30, or maybe even 20, years will be the densest part of Japan. It is one of the 'subcentres' the Japanese are trying to make around Tokyo, which in their opinion is too dense. This relatively small area will contain

1231

densities almost unimaginable to western eyes.

At Minato Mirai we saw the emergence of a particular building type, one we will soon have to recognize as the dominant typology: a completely inarticulate container with no architectural pretensions, whose only purpose is to accommodate certain processes or offices, and which simply represents a massive quantity of square metres imposed on an urban site without any more positive contribution.

Our scheme, to a large extent, had to complement this future city, or at least it had to be read in connection with it.

Key words : in play

(extract *S, M, L, XL*, 1996)

OPERA

Reiser and Umemoto

This project seeks to involve the opera house in the unique historical and spatial configuration of Cardiff's inner harbour by constituting the project as a series of infrastructural events. Regarding the opera house as infrastructure allows a redefinition of the nature and limits of the project at the extremes of scale, both as an integral part of the city and its environs and as a setting for a stage performance. The opera house, therefore, is not understood as an isolated monument, but as an open cultural form that would embody the same imperative and necessity as the docks, tunnels and roads that structure the harbour itself.

The concourse/foyer element is the crucial link between the exterior public spaces and the events in the opera house complex. A form is proposed that would maximize transparency and exchange between the piazza and concourse at the ground level, and between the auditorium and foyers above. This geodetic concourse/foyer divides into three tubes that insinuate themselves into the respective prongs of the theatre 'claw', becoming the lobby forms of the auditorium.

Current discussion regarding the tactics of achieving formal and programmatic heterogeneity, in the realm of architecture and planning, has occasioned a reassessment of spatial models and technologies heretofore relegated to the scrap heap of Utopian modernism. Among these discarded technologies stands the geometric and structural conception known as geodesics or geodetics. This project explores some of the architectural implications of geodetics, whose flexibility is capable of adapting to complex spatial formations without a corresponding increase in the complexity of the system. In geodetics exact geometries such as the dome are no more ideal than any number of geometric configurations. Moreover, the advent of computer-aided design and fabrication has obviated the technical difficulties encountered in earlier employments.

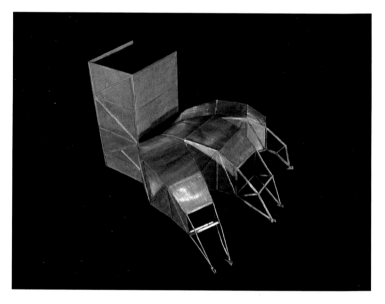

In geodetics many properties and possibilities can be found, mainly the skeletal model – structure and skin – and the structural skin model as a monocoque construction. However, in an expanded reading, however, geodetics acts as a structural tissue or flesh – an intermediate structure that would assemble heterogeneous agglomerations of space, program and path.

[Credits: Jesse Reiser + Nanako Umemoto; computer – Sean Daly; assistants – John Kelleher, Jun Takahashi, Taiji Miyasaka, Don Keppler, Terry Sarajan and Hideki Tamura; software – Softimage.]

Key words : per-form . re-production . work

PENNY SCREEN

Baratloo and Balch

Room divider: a component system dismantling and fracturing ambient light, with American pennies joining laser cut sheets of an industrial laminate – a composite of canvas impregnated with phenolic resin. This 'cheap' screen is a shadowy machine wall, an optical device transforming light and transformed by light. The partition is an incandescent tent-wall, glowing a deep ruby red when lit from behind; an amber plastic complicated by the surface impression of the warp and weft of the canvas in direct light. As a functional unit the character of the screen refers directly to the etymology of display: *dis* (apart) + *plicare* (to fold).

Key words : screen . set-up . skin . tie

PLAY TIME

Sanford Kwinter

The city, as Lewis Mumford used to claim, stands among the greatest technological achievements of humankind. The city to which he referred – leaving aside for the moment the difficult question of whether it is the one that persists with us – arguably remains not only possibly our greatest technical achievement but among our greatest cultural and political ones as well. Nobody would deny the systematic way in which the rise of 'the city' deformed human existence, multiplying and transforming to an exquisite degree the brutishness and suffering of daily life; previously unguarded from the indifferent and adverse unfoldings of nature, now only to be subsumed by the calamity and storming of unfettered economic rationality. This latter development, however, may in the end need to be seen as inevitable, following as it does from the city's undeniable status as a technological object, that is, as a new social assemblage of monstrous – indeed, unprecedented – complexity, yet one whose engine was never other than the purely and coldly economic. And yet, let us admit once and for all, analyses of this kind have never told us anything.

The emergence of the city may also be listed among the greatest emancipatory events of the post-Enlightenment era. The sheer social density of the great urban centres – or rather, the almost molecular instability caused by their free and uncontrolled build up – made possible a thing no less consequential than the political revolution, or at any rate, a type of insurrection never seen before: one both 'popular' in texture and dynamism yet also driven by philosophical ideas. This new 'alloy', made up of bourgeois intellectual discourse and proletarian mass deployment, could only have been forged from a crucible in which great concentrations of historical substance had come to exist in unusual compression. That crucible, of course, was nothing other than the early modern city. Such compression accelerated the dynamo of history, not only by multiplying the number of connections and interactions of elements (citizens, institutions and their mutually engendered affects) but by altering the quality of their interactions too. Just as historian and theorist drudges have not tired of reminding us of the uniquely economic aspects of the twin emergence of capitalism and the city, so now are we compelled to develop an alternative culture through which the psycho-erotic, the *ludic*, and the sovereign dimensions of the new subject, its new social space, and all that is both possible and unsanctioned in these, might be made intelligible.[1] As the present publication, as well as a recent issue of the New York journal *ANY* devoted to the question of play suggest, the field may propitiously be gathering today in a way that allows the posing of this ever-so-subtle new question.

Of course I do not expect many readers to believe the claim, that what we have to deal with here might actually be a new question. But 'play', I argue, is a new question, it is always new, just as it is always about delivering up the new. This is why in our work and our reflection, we as inventors of the material environment have no choice but to begin where the work of Donald Winnicott concludes. For without any doubt, play is a space with an action and influence of its own. This space itself opens up only when the small-minded bureaucratic query of whether one 'made something up, or found it in the world' has been banished, or more to the point, put out of play.[2] Play introduces an altogether different type of productivity (and one not limited to the human cultural world): it allows us a contractual suspension of the gravity of need, frees us of our ingrained meanness, and gives us the room to posit hypotheses that will not undergo verification by witless referees. Only in play do we today find the lost universe of pure truth.

But what does all this mean? Perhaps quite simply, that the product of true play has nothing essential to do with the objects and proclamations that appear to ensue from it, but rather with the invention of the entire alternative world from which those objects and proclamations are drawn. In other words, and there is absolutely no reason to shy away from it, play is directly connected to what was once the province of the sacred. Play is about world-making in the absence of verification, that is, not in any way poor science but rather a sustained assault on the *status quo* of subjugated and managed (and therefore debased) reality. It is the formal, revolutionary destruction of rational or productive time. This is why, for Georges Bataille, play was seen as belonging to those catastrophically expensive activities in which a culture participates through internal economic necessity, such as sex, war, dreaming, festival etc, while for Walter Benjamin, the activity of gambling (in French, *jouer*) may have permitted the industrial worker his only total emancipation from the insidiously deep logic of accumulation and subsumption dictated by workplace machines. Today, more than ever, the spirit and ethic of true play, as a destructive and wasteful activity, must re-emerge as a necessary ingredient in any encounter of human productive energy with the machine-like environment into which it is almost uniformly projected. Sacred space need mean nothing more than the space of sumptuary practice and exchange, the space of 'untimely' propositions in the Nietzschean sense, that is, of propositions which go so against the tenor of the times as to appear at once both threatening and almost unverifiable. Play represents an always new type of clearing; it might be seen as a type of Sabbath in the very deepest sense, the introduction of a lucid, non-productive time-form into a world of crude spatiality, of commerce, and of their relentless technological mastery. Play announces the always inchoate revolutionary project of a world in which events and history – and the cultivation of a thick duration – might one day take conceptual precedence over places and things. At any rate, play today can honestly exist only as an activity of sabotage, resistance and wanton neglect of a modern, de-sanctified world to which it is indifferent but which is not indifferent to it.

Many will happily see in these arguments little more than an apologia for the most traditional forms of theological investment in a transcendental state of grace. Yet nothing is further from the case. True play is the cultivation of a radical immanence, the unfolding of cultural, aesthetic, social and even mystico-erotic values based on no pre-existing principle whatever; all this and fully antagonistic to the onward march of economic rationality. Clearly, for play to be real, it must be exceedingly, gloriously expensive. After all, it is the wagering of existence in the name of a pleasure that is never yet renamed.

But what does the modern world know of such irresistible experience? Very little perhaps, but even that does not mean that we too have to forget. Everyone agrees that our new cities are but vessels of anomie, and even our philosophers (to wit Jean-Luc Nancy and Jean-Francois Lyotard) are themselves thoroughly dazzled and unable to seize the fugitive element. The emancipations of the modernist city have, before our eyes, become the nameless gray depredations of the present one. Yet what were – or could now be – these emancipations to us? Did not the city permit the explosive diversification of personality, raise the chance encounter to a sublimated art form, break the stranglehold of church and family on private practice and public morality? Did it not inject a critical dimension of 'play' into the social mechanism – in the double sense of 'free action' and 'a sanctified space of pure hypothesis' – did it not, in fact, eroticize the public sphere? The Greeks conceived of a life as an art form, but only in the modern city did it actually become so of necessity. Thus the city, to return to Bataille's exotic thesis, may be seen less as the place where wealth is accumulated and multiplied than the place where energy may be artfully – but profligately and wantonly – spent.

The ecstasy of play then, in the final analysis, has to do with its relationship to beauty. We say that we play music but never (yet!) that we play architecture. Yet the majesty of architecture (at least of non-classical types) is never revealed in its image but, like music, in the syncopations of its flow. The theatricality of architecture might actually be understood as an extra-dimension added on to the merely spatial (instrumental) world, the clearing, so to speak, of the speculative, transient, and fragile realm of play. Just as Greek drama emerged from the one-dimensional line (or half-circle) of the chorus, in order to individuate a specific possible world from the primordial substrate (the continuity of song), and just as its characters invariably fell back into this substrate in an ecstasy in which, only later, did we agonizingly recognize the unfolding of our own mortality, so now may we see play as an exquisite expression of our relenting to the tragic mode. To play is always to play with death, but at the same time to forge from this anxious proximity a link to beauty which could otherwise never be made. To play (to write a play? to take one in?) is, to borrow a phrase from Shakespeare's time, to 'laugh and lie down', to live a life or to give place to form in a transient, even momentary other world, and then to die out of it willingly and repeatedly – a world, a form, and a life neither 'found' nor 'made up', just lived in the full immediacy of death. To play is to give shape to what is beyond space, that is to

time itself, amid the full and tragic awareness of its waning, to deposit a figure in that which flees, and to know that its deliquescence (and unverifiability) is the lyrical condition of beauty.

Notes

1 Certainly by the late 19th century with the rise of philosophical sociology and scientific psychology, certain figures such as Durkheim, Simmel, Charcot and others had begun systematically to report the whole new metropolitan character that had already been exhaustively treated in the novel, in poetry and to a lesser extent, in painting. In the 20th century, outside of these 'artistic' modes, only Freud and Benjamin seem particularly notable.

2 On this critical question of legitimization and the ways it is elided by ritual, spontaneous play activity see Winnicott, *Play and Reality*, 1971, and Christian Hubert's discussion of this in 'Playtime', ANY, New York, October, 1995: extract printed below. Integral to this problem as well is the socio-historical and narrative modalities of the 'carnivalesque' most fully developed in the work of MM Bakhtin, *The Dialogical Imagination and Rabelais and his World*.

PLAYTIME

Christian Hubert

For theorists of the machine age, the progress of machine technology consisted in the elimination of play in a very literal sense. In his *Theoretische Kinematik* of 1875, Franz Reuleux described this correlation: 'the more primitive the technology, the less attuned the parts of the machine to each other, the greater the degree of play – the more perfected the technology, the closer the fit, the less play between the individual parts.' From the late 19th century on, the progress of machine technology was measured by the formation of great machine-like ensembles such as the railroad; every element of which fit together to minimize play and friction. The goal of eliminating play was not confined to overtly machine-like ensembles. The great processes of social rationalization, a kind of feedback process transforming society in the image of its own machine products, were based precisely on work, not play. After Max Weber, 'Rationalization' became the term used to describe not only social formation, but the value orientations of the personality, and the overall meaning structures of culture. Even in the psychoanalytic field, progress was understood in terms of the elimination of play, in the descriptions of childhood as a move from the pleasure principle to the reality principle. According to Freud, the infant's ego at first knows no boundaries and recognizes no external objects that escape its control. Later, the reality principle sets the boundaries between ego and world and allows the negotiation of deferred pleasure. In its first experiences of civilization and its discontents, the child learns that its wishes cannot always be fulfilled, that objects and persons exist outside the self, and that frustration is an inevitable, but manageable part of life. Insofar as play is understood in relation to pleasure, for Freud, then, accepting the reality principle is to forgo the pleasures of play and to accept the frustrations of work.

But when the prevailing views of modernity began to be revised during the 1960s, play became a privileged arena of alternative investigation. According to the great child psychologist Donald Winnicott, whose *Play and Reality* was published posthumously in 1971, play is central to the development of the psychological self. Although Winnicott accepted the Freudian schema in

the main, he accorded play the status of a semi-autonomous phase or 'transitional' state, between the pure pleasure principle and acceptance of the reality principle. For Winnicott, play is a psychological state where the boundaries between self and the world remain labile and fluid, a state which is important not only for the development of the child, but also has significant ramifications for human life and culture in general. In the state of play, objects can take on a paradoxical status. A bit of blanket, for instance, can become a 'transitional object', one that is neither fully part of the self nor an explicitly external object, neither thumb nor teddy bear. For Winnicott, play requires an acceptance of this paradoxical status, and he argues that this acceptance is the source of creativity and of human engagement in the cultural field.

Winnicott emphasizes that the space of play and its transitional objects must remain beyond the reach of a question he poses thus: 'Did you find that (in the world) or did you make it up?' This question is at the heart of my interest in play, and I would like to think about it both in terms of the question and in terms of the answer. What is at stake in this question? When is it appropriate to ask it? When is it better to reject or ignore it? When would the answer have to be both.

If the child psychologist refrains from asking this question, for fear of destroying the realm of play, this is precisely what critical culture asks of science 'Did you find that (in the world) or did you make it up?' It is the basis for all de-fetishizing or demystifying criticism that uncovers the work of 'naturalization' behind invented culture passing for found nature. It is the question that purports to differentiate human technology, the prime example of invention, from nature, the question the very asking of which forms the basis of culture. Today, this question and its use seems to divide cultural criticism, especially in its contemporary textual and social constructivist forms, from creative exploration, and I believe that it is only by accepting this paradox, by holding the question of finding or inventing in abeyance, that the pleasures of play can lead to the possibilities of other 'intermediate' cultural experiences that might include architecture.

Key words : play

BEEVOR MULL

Architects

Rmm/cmb.

Mr. J. Preston Esq.,
Planning Department,
Shire Hall,
Castle Hill,
Cambridge.
CB3 OAP

10th March 1995.

Dear Mr. Preston.

RE: QUADRATURA

As discussed at our recent meeting I write to outline the aims and methodology of the Quadratura project and the ways we would like to involve the planning process in them.

As you know the collaboration between Edward Allington and ourselves is mandated to examine the procedures and expectations that influence co-operation between architects and artists. The project centres on the creation of a fictional space which lies beyond the "ceiling" created in St. Peters Church.

This fictional world is partly described by models, drawings and the ceiling itself but we also feel it is crucial to generate a more widespread and potent myth of its potential existence. One of the ways we would like to do this is by the submission of a detailed planning application to Cambridge City Council. We see the application not as preparation for a further construction but as an end in itself. The application will generate the myth that such a space will or could exist. Its expression as a planning application authenticates it and allows it to compete in peoples imagination with other more everyday myths. Therefore in order for the project to enter the public imagination in a believable form we wish to make a real planning application and have it processed in the normal way.

As we explained the procedure for doing this is underway and is as follows:

We have now located ten sites in Cambridge which share the same datum level as the ceiling we will install in St.Peters Church. The owners of these spaces will become "angels" and will be invited to become part of the project. This will be done in two ways:

cont.

1 CHAPEL COURT , FERRARS ROAD , HUNTINGDON , CAMBS , PE18 6DH .
Tel: (0480) 454404 / 456589 .
Fax (0480) 413404 .

CATRINA M BEEVOR BA MA(RCA) RIBA . ROBERT M MULL Bsc (Hons) AA Dipl RIBA . Consultant ARTHUR.S MULL DA Dipl TP MRTPI RIBA

---

cont. 2

Firstly the angels will be eligible to visit (via a hoist) the space above the St.Peters Church ceiling and secondly we will seek their permission to become part of a planning application which will involve a change of use for a part of their property into an entry point into the fictional space described by the Quadratura project. In this way we create a new community of Cambridge citizens who have shared a common experience and who in effect own a part of the project. Although there are ten individual sites we would like them to be considered together as a single application and therefore to be covered by a single fee.

It would be our intention to submit the application in early April with the hope that it would be considered and if possible determined before the exhibition ends in late May. Within the context of the application we would like the church space to be considered as a 1:1 model of one "entry"point into the fictional space described by the project . Similarly the drawings supporting the application would be on display in the Architecture Gallery and could be viewed there by interested members of the public in much the same way that drawings of a conventional application can be viewed in your offices.

Lastly with regards to neighbour notification. As discussed if the project constitutes one application with ten parts then we are in effect describing a vast space and the problem of notification becomes enormous. Accordingly we would propose that neighbour notification is carried out via a feature in the Cambridge Evening News.

Since our meeting we have located the ten points and I enclose for your information a map which describes there spread. I also enclose the latest working drawing of the installation itself.

I hope the above description is sufficient for you to discuss the project with your colleagues. However should you require any further information I would be pleased to provide it.

Thank you for your help to date.

Yours sincerely,

R M Mull.

R.M.Mull
Beevor Mull Architects.

cc. Commissions East.

The Guildhall, Cambridge CB2 3QJ
Telephone: (0223) 463341/2
Extension: 2630
Facsimile: (0223) 463214
Minicom Direct Dial: (0223) 463219

**CAMBRIDGE
CITY COUNCIL**

Planning

Date: 19 April 1995

Robert Mull
Beevor Mull Architects
1 Chapel Court
Ferrars Rd
Huntingdon
Cambs PE18 6DH

Our ref: JKP/P56/2

Your ref:

Dear Mr Mull

"Quadratura", Cambridge

St Peter's Church; New Hall, Huntingdon Rd; ADC Theatre, Park St; Okinaga Room, St Edmund's College; Storey's House, Mount Pleasant; 10 Albion Row, Castle Hill; Chesterton Mill, French's Rd; Westminster College, Madingley Rd; H Langdon & Co, St Peter's St.

I refer to our discussions regarding the possible creation of accesses to a "mythical plane" intersecting the above properties, with the "Quadratura" installation in St Peter's Church being an illustrative full size scale model.

Permission may be required under the Planning Acts for the physical works involved in forming the proposed accesses. In considering any such works, you have to be mindful of the need to satisfy Building Regulations and safety requirements, where relevant.

Planning Permission may be required for works materially affecting the external appearance of the buildings; this would be a matter for assessment in each individual case. Any application for planning permission would have to be accompanied by the appropriate fee; any planning application made for work which does not need permission will be returned.

Listed Building Consent would be required for any works (external or internal) affecting the character of the following buildings which are listed:

St Peter's Church	listed	Grade B
New Hall		Grade II*
Chesterton Mill		Grade II
Westminster College		Grade II

Assessment of whether listed building consent is required will involve consideration of the effect of the proposed works on both the physical fabric of the building and on its character. No fee is required for listed building consent applications.

Peter Studdert B Arch RIBA DipTP MRTPI Director of Planning

Working for the Community

Printed on Recycled Paper

The process of assessment in relation to listed building consent is best illustrated by considering the "full size scale model" within the Church. The installation will greatly change the perceived character of the interior of the Church, but only for the duration of the exhibition. Perhaps most importantly, it has been established in the initial consultations that no additional structure is needed, as the existing beams are adequate to take the additional load of the hoist. The installation will be simply hung on the existing beams, with no fixings to the fabric of the listed building. The installed "plane" is to be lightweight involving no significant fixings. Consequently, the proposed "model" will involve no alterations to the existing fabric, and will be completely reversible as well as being of strictly limited duration; considering these factors together, it is my view that listed building consent will not be required for the installation within the Church. (Had it been necessary to install a loadbearing floor capable of supporting the weight of an "angel", listed building consent would have been required).

Applications will only be accepted if they include information to show the full impact of the proposal on the character of the building in question, as required by government guidance (Planning Policy Guidance Note 15: Planning and the Historic Environment).

Any application(s) which are received will be subject to the normal consultation procedures. Neighbours would be notified; and applications affecting listed buildings or conservation areas would be advertised accordingly. All the proposed locations are within a conservation area, apart from New Hall, Chesterton Mill, and St Edmund's College (which adjoins the conservation area boundary). Individual formal consultation of all owners or occupiers of properties within the area of the "mythical plane" would be unnecessary in terms of application(s) relating to particular sites as well as being both expensive and extremely impractical; should such consultation be considered desirable, it would be for the applicant to arrange a feature in the "Town Crier" or "Cambridge Weekly News", which would appear to be the best way to reach all the properties.

Any applications will be considered in relation to the policies of the Development Plan (the Cambridgeshire Replacement Structure Plan), and other material considerations including Government Guidance (PPG 15) and the Consolidated Draft Cambridge Local Plan.

Yours sincerely

J Preston
CONSERVATION AND DESIGN OFFICER

QUADRATURA

Angel 1

Julia Theophilus
Collected 10.03.95
Location 1. 0-2 degrees
Catering manager
New Hall
Huntingdon Road
Cambridge

Angel 2

John West
Collected 10.03.95
Location 1. 3-4 degrees
Security
Okinaga Room
St Edmund's College
Cambridge

Angel 3

Joyce Mcnab
Collected 4.03.95
Location 1. 0-6 degrees
Storeys House
Mount Pleasant
Cambridge

Angel 4

Michael Peacock
Collected 10.03.95
Location 1. 6-8 degrees
10 Albion Yard
Castle Hill
Cambridge

Angel 5

Peter French
Collected 5.03.95
Location 1. 77 degrees
Mill House
Chesterton Mill
Frenches Road
Cambridge

Angel 6

Toby Ducker
Collected 4.03.95
Location 1. 156-158 degrees
ADC Theatre
Park Street
Cambridge

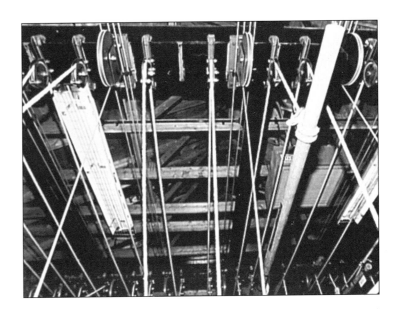

QUADRATURA

DATUM: (ceiling)
The infinite datum set by the ceiling of St Peter's Church, Cambridge

ANGEL SITES: (ceiling)
Remote sites cut by the 'ceiling' established by the infinite datum (entry points to the imaginary space).

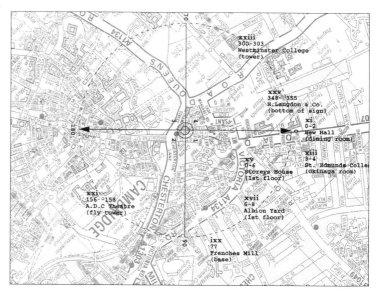

CEILING: (portal) St Peter's Church
The entry point into the imaginary space (Quadratura)

Key words : act out . illusion . make believe

James Williamson

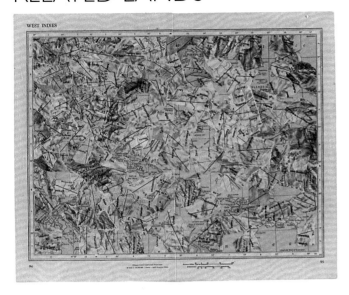
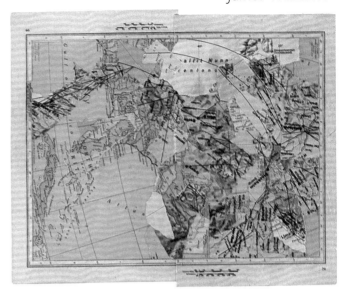
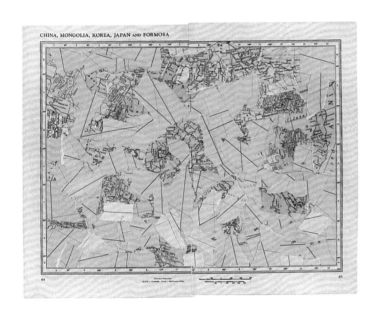
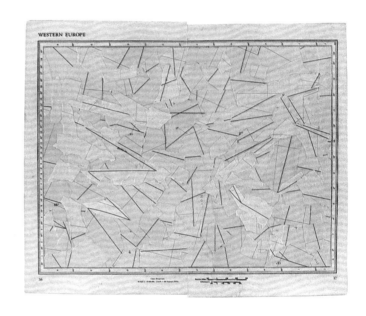
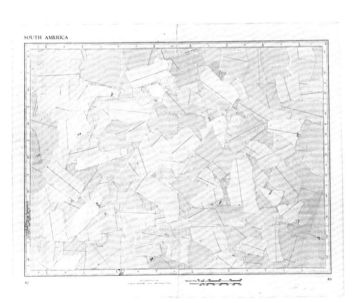

Key words : frontier . re call . skin . territory

REMAINDER, THE

. . . a Parable

Legend has it that the French painters, Corot and Courbet, used to go on painting expeditions together. Corot, the heir of the Romantic landscape painters, spent hours choosing the place where he would eventually set up his easel: the prospect had to be just right, the landscape must compose itself before he attempted to put it on canvas. When this long and painful process had ended, Courbet, the realist, turned his back on him and started painting whatever was to be seen on the other side. This is my aim: to describe the other side of language. The grammarian and the linguist but also the philosopher of language, choose their objects carefully. The first simplifies in order to formulate clear rules, the second separates the relevant from the irrelevant phenomena, the third is intent on saving rational communication and therefore on ridding natural language of the various impurities that obscure it. These are the frontiers that the remainder subverts and that I wish to cross. I shall dwell in the exceptional and the agrammatical, in the irrelevant and the excluded aspects of language, in the ambiguities and impurities of natural idioms. A countryside less imposing perhaps, and certainly more difficult to paint, but every inch as fascinating as the ordered landscapes of science.

(extract *The Violence of Language*, 1990)

Key words : remainder

ROAD BED S

One Alphabet for the Road

eɪ   is for   **a**dults [] snapped up by the ground comma fall[ing] no longer understand 1
       1 + G Deleuze =

bi: is for   **b**etraying repetition [] of bodies which [] cut and bruise [] on roadbeds 2
       2 + L Bersani + G Deleuze + J Kerouac =

si: is for   **c**ondensing [] step[s] on Asphalt [] which repeat [] and distance previous moves 3
       3 + Mastic Asphalt Handbook + L Bersani =

di: is for   **d**riving at night [] staring into the head[]lights [] overtaken by a house 4
       4 + L Anderson + W Wenders =

i: is for   **e**vents sought [] at the surface [] which redden [] and become [] green 5
       5 + JG Ballard + G Deleuze =

ɛf   is for   **f**ree[ing] the mouth to speak [] at the mouth of the road 6
       6 + G Deleuze =

dʒeɪ   is for   **g**ravel [] trapped [] in black semisolid substances [] in parts of America 7
       7 + Collins English Dictionary =

eɪtʃ   is for   **h**istory teach[ing] us that sound [] roads [] and bedside furniture [] have no foundation 8
       8 + G Deleuze + W Wenders =

aɪ   is for   **i**dentif[ying] and [dis]unif[ying] vast spaces and separate buildings 9
       9 + J Galbraith =

dʒeɪ   is for   **j**ack [] joker and [] an imaginary number 10
       10 + Collins English Dictionary =

keɪ   is for   a thin slice of [] surface [] scratched and rubbed in blac**k** 11
       11 + R Kipling =

ɛl   is for   **l**ines at the surface [] which tie together [] erogenous zones 12
       12 + G Deleuze =

ɛm   is for   **m**obile homes [] at home and on the road at the same time 13
       13 + W Wenders =

Instructions for fabrication
Select a road. Look at it and forget it at the same time. Imagine it to be continuous. Imagine it to travel as far as the eye can see. Because it is forgettable photograph it. Divide the road by the camera 26 times. Cut

ɛn   is for   neo organic [] roadside [] motifs in walnut formica 14
                 14 + *Architect's Journal* =

əʊ   is for   one for the road [] one after an other 15
                 15 +

pi: is for   paralysed by fear [] on the road [] at night staring into the headlight 16
                 16 + J Kerouac + W Wenders =

kju: is for   questions of [] addish comma subtrac comma and multiplica tion 17
                 17 + L Carroll =

ɑ: is for   roadbeds comma where surfacial forms disfigure and fictions [] are in flux 18
                 18 + Heraclitus =

ɛs   is for   sheets [] of Asphalt [] rolled [] in the wrong way 19
                 19 + Mastic Asphalt Handbook =

ti: is for   turning right comma left and straight 20
                 20 +

ju: is for   unequalled faultless [] surfaces []stretching and []buckling 21
                 21 + *The Architectural Review* =

vi: is for   virtually using roads which [] start when they start and stop when they stop 22
                 22 + M Serres + L Carroll =

ʲd√bᵊliju: is for   winter comma when the [] sheets [] are white [] and Asphalt [] reddens 23
                 23 + L Carroll + M A Handbook + G Deleuze =

ɛks   is for   []xcuse me comma can you tell me where I am [] 24
                 24 + L Anderson =

waɪ   is for   yes and [] an unspecified no period of things 25
                 25 + Collins English Dictionary =

zi: is for   zzz... 26
                 26 +

the unending road into pieces and bits. Identify where the surface of the roadbed stops and where the surface of the photograph begins. Cut the surface. Look at it. Now imagine the bed you have made. Lie on it.
Key words : dream . distortion . illusion . land . surface

ROW HOUSES

Houston, Texas

1992 (summer): Houston artist Rick Lowe discovers an abandoned lot of 22 identical shotgun houses in the city's predominantly African - American Third Ward.

Shotgun House: One room wide, one storey tall, several rooms deep, has its primary entrance in the gable end, has no hallway. (A bullet can be shot through the front door and will exit through the back door without piercing any walls.)

Shotgun House: Introduced in the US by free Haitians who settled in New Orleans after the Haitian slave rebellion (early 19th century). Transformed by Caribbean and European building techniques the shotgun house never the less expresses the enduring social values and cultural traditions of generations of African-Americans.

Shotgun House: A symbol of unity and cultural continuity.

The Third Ward: Designated a 'pocket of poverty' (City of Houston Redevelopment Plan, 1986).

1993: Lowe realises that the site was a setting in which work by African-American artists could be produced and experienced, providing a powerful link to the past, saving the buildings. A non-profit organisation: Project Row Houses was established to obtain a five year lease on the property, rescuing them from demolition with the help of hundreds of volunteers.

Under the umbrella of a local arts organization, Diverse Works, Project Row Houses is awarded $25,000 seed money from the National Endowment for the Arts (NEA) in addition to $41,000 from arts foundations.

Deborah Grotfeldt, assistant director of Diverse Works joined Lowe full time as managing director. Lowe began renovating the first house himself. It became clear that the scope of the project could be extended. The plan to use ten houses as sites for installations grew to include the renovation of the remaining twelve as low-income housing.

1994 (April): Two houses restored. Boarded over windows were painted as a 'Drive-By Exhibit'. Fourth year students at the University of Houston, directed by Sheryl Tucker, exhibit a proposal for a vegetable / sculpture garden.

The owner of the site defaults on his loan – foreclosure proceedings are initiated. This action renders Project Row Houses lease / purchase agreement invalid.

Patrons of the arts, Isaac and Sheila Heimbinder, offer a loan of $100,000 to purchase the property outright.

Amoco Corporation gives over 400 corporate workers the day off to restore the exterior of houses that are designated for housing and community services.

Home Depot donate building materials.

Chevron furnish seven houses to be used for low-income housing.

Houston Museums – the Menil Collection and the Museum of Fine Arts, Trinity Methodist Church and individual patrons sponsor the gallery spaces.

October: The installations open to the public.

1995 (April): Second round of installations opens.

NEA awards $27,000 for Project Row Houses second year of operation. Additional support is committed by the Cultural Arts Foundation of Houston and the Texas Commission on the Arts.

Project Row Houses raises $400,000 to fund art and cultural education programmes and The Young Mothers' Residential Programmes.

Seven families will move into renovated, furnished houses. The Meadows foundation awards $100,000; families participate in counselling, training and childcare programmes in the project's daycare centre and after school programmes.

The project encompasses the production of art, art and cultural education, historic preservation, neighbourhood revitalization and community service.

1996: The project continues.

Key words : in-play . negotiation . ordinary

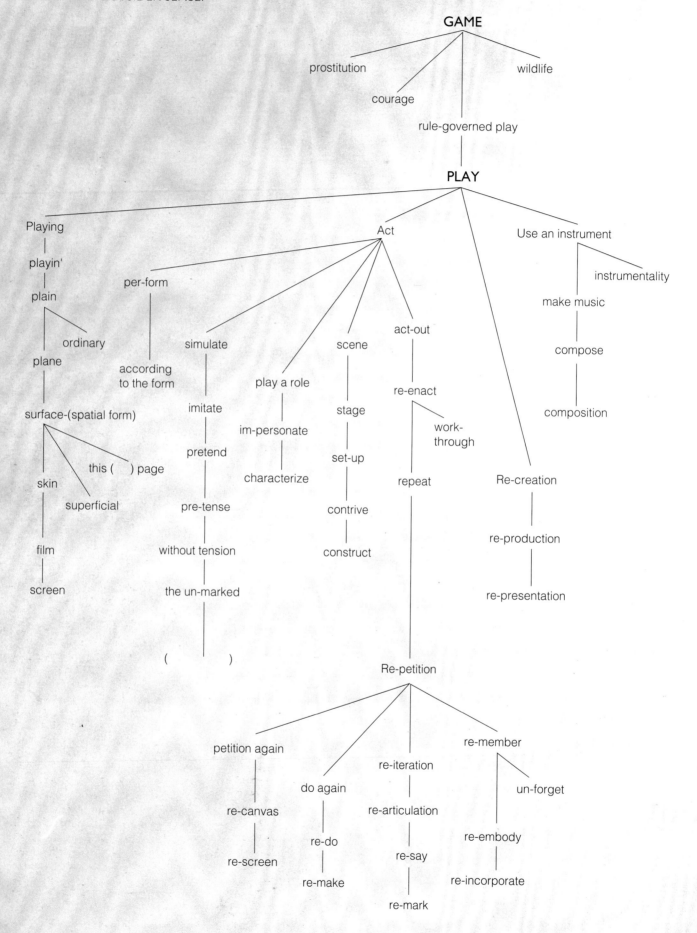

Introduction: An Architectural Tale

A being finds itself at the top of a long flight of stairs.
Slowly, taking time, its vision traverses the space,
till it comes to rest, at the point of termination,
on a beloved object.

What does the being see?

The beloved object.

But is this all?

A being finds itself at the top of a long flight of stairs.
Slowly, taking time, its vision traverses the space . . .

And thereby is seen,
not just the point of termination, a Her,
but that which is-terminated, a nOt Her,
the space (in) itself.

This tale shows that presence is composed of two elements, the density of (what) matter('s) as it inheres in a beloved object, and the in-density of the space which surrounds and flows through this. Though we may have density without space as in black holes, or space without density as in vacuums, for the purposes of everyday life Being always exhibits both density and space. (These terms are not technical, merely descriptive.) In other words, we do not live in a world in which the opposition presence/absence can be neatly mapped onto the opposition matter/space, for space is a part of presence, and that which is truly absent is what has neither matter nor space. Presense is not therefore an irreducible atomic element, but a complex composed of two principles. The philosophical consequences of this observation are rather large, for it forces us to accept pantheism, as opposed to the current monotheism which currently worships the signifier as the signifier of what matter's only. However the purpose of this essay is to discuss its ramifications for visual recreation, the point being that, like philosophy, the arts are also imbued with a thoroughgoing monotheism that worships the mark on the page as the signifier of some 'thing' which matter's.

But where does this leave space, the other aspect of Being's presence? What signifier refers us to this? The answer to this question, as shown on the diagram of associations, is surprisingly simple: the page itself on which the representing one inscribes their (re)marks. It is an almost universally forgotten fact, at least in western culture, that the blankness of the page is itself one of the signs in any descriptive system, be this visual or verbal. For want of any other explanation, we could propose that this f-act of forgetting stems from western culture's obsession with work, for when we begin with a playin', as in the diagram above, it quickly becomes apparent that this (   ) plane is itself a sign. It seems that when we lose the recognition of this playin' sign we also lose conscious knowledge of what it refers to, the free-play of that which is s-pace.

In western descriptive systems the blankness of the unmarked page is seen as the 'natural' signifier of the space between things. But if real space is tangible or present then it has properties of its own that are not arbitrary. The question must then be asked as to whether the properties of the blank page are adequate to the representation of this space, ie, whether a blank page is indeed the 'natural', or even a good enough signifier of the presence of space? There is one class of composers for whom this is clearly not the case, the so-called 'Outsider' artists who fill up the spaces between the solid objects in their representations with endlessly repeated motifs.

Does this mean these peculiar subjects actually 'see' in space structures the rest of us cannot recognize? Or does it mean rather that they don't take for granted the assumed naturalness of the singifying relation between the blank page and space; ie, they don't conform to the socially constructed assumption that the blank page is the natural sign of space, just as some psychotics don't accept the penis as the natural sign of the difference between the sexes? And if, as I will argue, this latter is the case, how then do these subjects re-present their sense of space? If for them the plane is not plain, how do they make a play in it? In order to answer this question we must first look at some theories of representation and/or signification and the way this phenomenon inheres in the human form of being.

On the Discrepancy between Language and Langue

In his book *Philosophy Through the Looking Glass*, Jean-Jacques Lecercle analyses what he calls reflexive delirium, or 'delire'. According to Lecercle, this way of using language, practised by Carroll, Artaud, Roussel, Brisset, Schreber and other *fous litteraires*, lies on the border between the dominant tradition of socially controlled instrumental language and the completely unintelligible babbling of the truly alienated. Delire is a special form of discourse where 'the old philosophical question about the emergence of sense out of non-sense recieves a new formulation.'

As Lecercle points out however, in general those who practice this mode of language-use are not professional philosophers or linguists. Rather, they are ones for whom the matter and space of language, its phonetic substantiality and its formal structures, are not simply tools to be used for the expression of some other experience, but are themselves felt as real 'objects' of experience. The problem for these ones is that the language they are given to express their experience of being-in-language is felt to be inadequate. In other words, they are subjects for whom the French distinction between language as the generalized intellectual faculty of re-presentation or signification, the forms and contents of thought in itself, and language as langue, the idealized systems of the 'natural' languages we are given to express this, is felt particularly acutely. What we have in these cases are concrete examples of the well known fact that langues are idealized systems which only imperfectly capture the nature of language, for to these subjects their given langue is constantly experienced as radically inadequate to the expression of their sense of being-in-language.

Naturally such subjects are of immense interest to philosophers of language because they expose precisely where the discrepancies between our langues (natural languages) and language, the faculty of thought, mind or psyche 'in-itself', lie. As Lecercle says, in the work of such writers language is both 'liberated' from the systematic rules of its structure, a langue, 'and dominant, for in these cases, it is no longer the individual subject who uses (L)anguage for their own purpose, but (L)anguage itself which imposes its workings on the subject, who thereby loses mastery.' Instead of using a langue instrumentally, instead of being the masters of a langue, these unique beings become subjected to language, and thereby they become the instruments through which language plays itself out. Instead of being the play-ers they become the instruments upon, or with which, language itself plays.

These subjects show us that though we may use a langue instrumentally to express something about the external world, every utterance, every re-presentation we make in a langue, also necessarily refers to our own representational faculty, ie, to language, whether we intend it or not, for in order to use any langue at all a being must first have incorporated or been captured by language. This point has been made often enough in the past 100 years of linguistic theory, by Saussure, Barthes, Derrida, Lacan, etc. What is interesting about the *fous litteraires* is that for these particular subjects the duplicity of language is not simply theoretical, but is experienced as a real lie, for to these ones the langues they have been given are found to be seriously wanting in their capacity to re-present being-in-language.

This last point is of profound significance, for the usual philosophical line is that the discrepancy between real-life experience (in this case, of language) and langue arises because there is a surfeit of signifiers and not enough real objects to match these. But what the *fous litteraire* show is that the problem lies in exactly the opposite direction, namely, a lack in the signifiers and a surfeit of the real, for to these extraordinarily sharp ones it is the langue which fails, not the reality of being-in-language. Their problem is not that they have too many signs and nothing to attach them to, but that they are engaged in real experiences for which none of the signs currently on offer seems adequate. By thus highlighting the limits or inadequacies of our current descriptive systems, the *fous litteraires* confront us with the limits of our knowledge, ie, with the fact that our knowledge, which is simply our capacity to re-present experience, is lacking with respect to the particular experience of being-in-language.

Of course this raises the question as to whether there is not something about the experience of being-in-language that is inherently unsignifyable, or unrepresentable? But, whereas 20th-century theoreticians seem content to accept such a limitation, the *fous litteraires* are not. And in their forcing of the limits of langues in their attempts to overcome this barrier, they compel us all to see that perhaps it is not quite so absolute as we might imagine. They show us that, even if it can be demonstrated there is some absolute limit to the representablity of our being-in-language, we are a long way from that point yet. One is reminded here of the believers in a flat earth, for we cannot help but suspect that those who pronounced most vociferously on the world's end, where everything falls off the edge and ceases to be, were precisely the ones who never went any where near that edge. On the other hand, it was precisely those who did attempt to approach this limit who discovered it did not exist, at least not in that form. For if there is a limit to this earth, it is not of the kind which can be described by a cut in a plane. Similarly, one suspects that if there is a limit to langues' capacity to represent our being-in-language it is also not of the type envisioned by the proponents of representational impossibility theory. At the very least, the work of the *fous litteraires* compels us to keep an open mind on this subject, and not write-off our langues before we have fully explored what they can do.

The Outsider's Vision of this Discrepancy
The same discrepancy also haunts the visual mediums, for these too are langues, whether they use three or only two dimensions of space.

Perhaps the main difference between visual and verbal langues is that, whereas most of us, in using them purely instrumentally, believe verbal langues are adequate to the representation of our thought, when it comes to visual langues, particularly those which operate in only two dimensions, we are all too abundantly aware of the discrepancy between how we know we visually experience the world in our mind's I, and how we may re-represent this externally, in an image on a surface. In fact this discrepancy is also manifest in our verbal descriptive systems, but we are not so aware of it then because we aren't aware in verbal descriptions of even the need to describe space. This is probably because we regard verbal langues as linear, ie, one-dimensional, and hence as not being about space at all. Though this assessment has to be proved, not assumed, the fact that all visual descriptive systems employ at least two dimensions, forces our attention on space in a way verbal systems do not.

So, in visual langues we immediately become aware of the fact that we have to translate what we believe is really a three-dimensional phenomenon, our experience of being-in-space, into a representation that includes only two dimensions. The inadequacy of this translation of one experience of space into another imposes itself upon us with a force that is often totally debilitating. Unable

to deal with the discrepancy between what they want to say and the apparent inability of the visual langue to allow such an expression, many people are simply reduced to 'silence'. Even when not completely debilitating, this discrepancy, between a being's real visual experience of the world, its visual language and the idealized systems or visual langues offered for the external representation of this, has disabling effects, for it causes distortions in our actual experience.

In western culture the discrepancy between the lived experience (of the language) of space and the array of devices offered for the representation of this in our langues, both visual and verbal, is vast. The effect of this inadequacy is to compel a focus of attention on 'things', or 'matter', to the detriment of the space around them which is now seen as simply an emptiness, ie, as the ab-sense of some-thing (else), rather than as a pre-sense in its own right. This one-sided focusing of attention manifests itself in both our representations and our actual experiences. That is to say, the inadequacy of our descriptive systems not only causes a distortion in our representations, it also causes a distortion in our conscious knowledge of actual experience, for without a sign with which to signify space to ourselves, we are unable to be conscious of having an experience of it at all. In this case, we are mastered, not by language, but by a langue, for it is langue alone, in providing the signs with which we can re-present our experience to ourselves, that is our consciousness of that experience. It is precisely against this tyranny of inadequate langues that many Outsiders so vigorously rebel.

Though most of us are content to accept that space is simply the ab-sense of some-thing (else), the signifier for which is the unmarked 'blank' of the inscribing surface, many Outsiders are not, for in their representations the spaces between objects (what matters) have as much presence as the objects themselves. In fact, one often has the impression that in these works no real distinction is made between these two aspects of being. Again, the problem is not an excess of signifiers and a lack in the real, but a surfeit of the real and an inadequacy in the socially ordained representational devices, for it is only their perception of the inadequacy of the blank page as a signifier of space's multifarious properties that enables Outsider artists to search for other ways of representing their experience of this phenomenon. The problem then becomes one of determining the generalized strategies by which these composers seek to overcome this lack in the available signifying material, the strategies by which they develop other signifiers for an experience which even they can only be dimly conscious of, however much their un-conscious knowledge of it may be pressing heavily on their being.

Strategies of Re-presentation
As treatises on the subject repeatedly show, the same methods are used by writers of delire and by outsider visual artists:

Rule-boundedness: rigid adherence to a set of apparently arbitrary rules governing both the production of primary elements and the combination of these.

Reiteration: obsessive repetition of a limited number of motifs, whose combinations alone form the overall composition.

Intentionality: the sense that though each individual gesture is arbitrarily executed and placed, the composition as a whole is imbued with deliberate intention.

Systematization: the sense that a definite system underlies and ultimately determines the placement of every mark, ie, that the composition is in-formed by a coherent underlying pattern or structure, even if the order individual marks are laid down in only reveals this slowly. (This not dissimilar to so-called chaos maths where a tightly structured pattern can emerge from an apparently random placing of individual marks.)

Non-hierarchicality: in the composition no single point is the focus of attention, all parts being equally significant,

Proliferation, even excess of meaning: the sense that even the tiniest elements of the composition are over-determined in significance, irrespective of whether this is interpretable by the viewer,

Playfulness: a willingness to use any means to achieve the required effect, irrespective of whether these are commonly utilized in this way or not.

When speaking to the makers of such compositions, they invariably express the view that what they are describing is a literal translation of something actually seen. In other words, these artists are not engaged in an act of creation *ex nihilo*, but are re-creating something they have already in some sense experienced. They are playing with a re-presentation of something already conceived of, not attempting to present us with something that is in itself 'original', though its effects may be highly original.

The combined effect of these techniques is to produce compositions in which there is a marked lack of distinction in the treatment of figure and ground, objects and space. As a result of regarding all elements as equally significant and of applying the same rules to the representation of all experiences, space can also be treated as (a) tangible, as being-present, not just as the absence of some (other) thing or presence. In other words, it is because they do not make an a prior decision that some experiences must be represented differently than others, but treat all experiences as equally subject to the same rules of interpretation, that these composers are able to signify space with the same signs used for the signification of the things that matter's.

We should be careful to note, however, that this equality with which signs are applied does not of itself indicate that no distinction is made between the experience of space and the experience of what matter's. After all, one's experience of being in love is radically different from the experience of say eating a ham sandwich, yet we commonly use the same basic set of signifiers to represent both these. Paradoxically, it is precisely because they don't have a unique sign for representing the experience of space that Outsider artists are able to represent it so well. It is rather the rest of us, in having accepted the blank page as its unique sign, who fail to say anything of significance about this experience, just as having the 'empty place' as the (only) sign of femininity enables us to effectively say nothing about this kind of being.

The Signifier

The above analysis may seem to imply that, in rejecting the blank page as the natural sign of what 's-pace, Outsider artists are whole-heartedly rejecting a superfluous sign. It may therefore seem to corroborate the contemporary linguist's belief in the surfeit of signifiers, for these subjects appear to demonstrate the non-necessity of one particular signifier. But this is merely an appearance, for the fact that they do not regard the blank page as the natural, or even as a sufficient, sign of space, does not mean they don't use it as a sign at all. To return to the analogy with the woman, just because someone does not regard 'silence', or the emptiness of speech, as the only appropriate representation of the feminine mode of being-subjected does not mean they do not have moments of silence in their own discourse. In order to speak, or write, at all we must put 'gaps' between our words, or else they would not be distinguishable from each other. But we do not ordinarily take every such gap as a necessary reference to a woman, ourselves or any other. These gaps are an intrinsic part of the structures of language which may be used to refer to many different phenomenon.

Outsiders use the blankness of the page as one part of the structuring devices of their visual langues. They just don't regard this particular device as being necessarily tied to a particular experiential phenomenon, ie, they don't regard as it as equivalent to a proper name, as do most of us. Rather, they see it as a structural part of language which may be used in making representations of many different phenomena. It's rather like lines in drawing which cannot be assumed to refer to one class of phenomenon alone, for, in the context of the drawing as a whole, they can be used to represent all manner of things, and yet still be seen as simply lines if isolated from their general context.

Of course this raises the question of whether or not there are some special signs which are not just general structuring devices, like lines, but which are, like proper names, in some way intrinsically tied to very specific phenomena? This is the idea that lies behind Lacan's notion of the signifier. But here we confront a fact of linguistic theory, namely that the same term can be used to designate different phenomena in different philosophies. The term 'signifier' is a specific case of such differential use.

In the semiotic theory of Ferdinand de Saussure all representations are seen as being composed of basic components called 'signifiers' which refer to, or re-present, concepts external to themselves called 'signifieds'. The whole relational unit of the signifier and the signified together, he called the 'sign'. In this theory, all representations, all signs are basically equivalent. But in Lacan's theory, the term 'signifier' is used to distinguish one very special class of representation, those which, in representing only language itself, do not in his view refer to any external reality, and hence do not have 'signifieds' at all. Such isolated signifiers are clearly not signs in the Saussurean sense, because they do not have signifieds. Lacan used the term 'representation' to refer to those signifiers which, in referring to something external to language, do have signifieds, and are therefore signs in the Saussurean sense. Thus, whereas Saussure made no distinctions between signs, Lacan did make one. This goes a long way short of the American philosopher Charles Peirce whose semiotics includes 310 different kinds of sign, but it is a beginning.

So we have two different uses of the same term. For Saussure the term 'signifier' is the name of all pieces representing material, words, images, etc. For Lacan it designates only those pieces signifying material, words, images, gestures, etc, which specifically signify a being's confrontation with its own re-presentational capacities, ie, its own being-in-language. Thus, whereas for Saussure, all signifiers have signifieds, and hence all signifiers make a reference to something other than themselves, for Lacan the term signifier refers only to those signifiers that are empty of reference, for they do not refer to anything beyond themselves, ie, the structure of representation as a thing in itself.

Amongst signifiers, Lacan further distinguished what he called 'The' or 'Master Signifier' as that signifier which represents the specific experience of Being-confronted with the limits of language, ie, the limits of one's own capacity to re-present one's experience to and of oneself. According to Lacan, what makes this experience of confronting the limit of our own re-presentational capacities so special is that, along with the sense of not-being-able-to-say, there is also the sense of a compulsion to say this; a compulsion to articulate precisely what is beyond articulation, namely what (I)'s un-subjected to language, ie, I's being-in-Itself. But, according to Lacan, the sense that there is any being-un-subjected to language is itself the principal effect of being-in-language, for outside language we cannot verify that any such state exists at all. Hence, the sense of what is beyond or outside language is itself a part of language. This is what the signifier represents, that limit which is both in-language, and yet somehow simultaneously beyond it.

We begin to see why the blank space may have a special status after all, for asserting the significance of the 'blankness' is perhaps one way of trying to articulate that which is seemingly both inarticulate and inarticulatable. I would personally argue that it is a very inadequate way of dealing with the problem, but that is another issue. What is not disputable is that, whatever means we use to express this point of impossibility in our experience of being-articulate, it is categorically not the same as the experience of being-in-space, which is, as the Outsiders show, articulatable with quite ordinary signs. One of the great virtues of Outsider art is thus that it uncouples the experience of the impossible point of being-in-language from the experience of being-in-space. In so doing, this art helps to refine our sense of precisely what the impossible experience of being-in-language is.

One could perhaps return to the analogy of the woman and suggest that this is another example of a lack of precision in our sense of the impossibility in our own articulate being, for the point(!) of the feminine mode of subjection may not be the same as the point of articulatable impossibility, though current analytic theory would have us believe that it is. However, Outsider art does manage to uncouple the experience of being-in-space from this impossibility, and thereby both widens the field of general phenomena we can adequately represent to ourselves and helps to focus our attention more closely on the specific nature of the phenomenon we find impossible to represent adequately; ie, the experience of being compelled to say that which is by definition beyond articulation. It would thus be true to say that for these subjects this is the point of all (their) representations.

What can we learn from this method, this attitude?

The Unconscious as Outsider

Taken as a whole, the use of the techniques outlined above creates a process something like a game, for games are rule-governed intentional systems in which the reiteration and recombination of a limited number of simple moves or pieces produces structures that are playable, full of significance and may be non-hierarchical. The only overt difference between the Outsider artists' process of play, or re-creation, and that of any other game is that most games do not purport to be re-presentations of some other experience, but are regarded as the experience in itself. However, as many studies have shown, a good many games are based on other life-experiences, above all, the experience of conflict. Games are, in many cases, ritualized ways of enacting conflicts we would otherwise have no way of working through. They are thus, like Outsider art, a way of using representations to re-create real problems in order to work these through in a manner not otherwise possible. Another process which uses repetitive representations to recreate problems in need of being worked through, especially problems caused by an inability to symbolize or signify some experience, is psychoanalysis.

As a clinical experience, rather than a purely philosophical theory, psychoanalysis is the process of trawling through the unconscious field in order to bring to consciousness those painful experiences we have so far been unable to digest because of a disordering, or mis-cognition, of the signs by which these could be re-presented, re-cognized, and so worked through. In this case, the cure must in some sense be the reverse of the cause, for the disordered or mis-cognized signs can only be re-cognized if the mechanism by which the disordering or mis-cognition came into being is undone, rather as we have to play a tape backwards in order to get out the twists and knots which distort its sound. But perhaps a better analogy would be that of playing an instrument, an action we only learn to execute well by constant repetition of precisely those elements we fail most dismally at.

According to Freud, the unconscious is composed of a system of gaps that have come into (the) being by various mechanisms:

Repression; because the being does not wish to acknowledge its awareness of some fact. This is a form of deliberate forgetting.

Dissolution; whereby the being severs connections between facts (images or other thoughts), so as not to acknowledge associations between them.

Invalid Inference; whereby the being makes (up) a conclusion that cannot validly be drawn from the premise it assumes.

Isolation; in which an event in memory is removed from its context.

Non-Comprehension; in which a being fails to remember an experience consciously because it either mis-cognizes that experience, or fails to recognize that it had it at all.

All these acts, and they are acts (even the non-comprehension) produce gaps in conscious memory. The totality of these gaps is what Freud called the unconscious. Thus, all these acts are mechanisms of subjection, for to be-subjected is to be subjected to the unconscious, that is to a 'gap' in conscious representation or recreation. Subjection, in Freud's view, is the sense of an inability or gap in the being's capacity to re-create itself in the field of representation. The unconscious is thus simply the sense of subjection to this gap, and its contents are not arbitrary because they manifest themselves in a very definite fashion, namely through a species of repetition. What we cannot remember consciously, what we cannot consciously represent to ourselves we are destined to repeat, but repeat in a very specific sense, namely, through acting it out.

As we have seen, Outsiders are subjects who particularly focus on, and hence endlessly repeat, the point of impossibility all beings experience when confronted with the limits of their own re-creational or re-presentational capacities. The question is then, to which of Freud's unconscious mechanisms are such people most subjected?

From the above analysis of their work, we may propose that Outsiders, whether poets or imagists, are beings subjected to the particular form of non-comprehension which results when one has either mis-cognized or failed to cognize altogether the experience of being-incorporated into language, for this is what they are destined to go on repeating or re-enacting time and time again. Paradoxically, it is precisely these subjects who have failed to cognize the experience of incorporating language adequately who show us what it really is. One proof of this fact is that, as pointed out, they are exceptionally good at distinguishing what it is not, for example, that it is not the same as the experience of being-in-space.

The rest of us, in whom the re-cognition of this experience has been adequately performed, having no need to re-enact the experience, also have no real knowledge of it as we usually know next to nothing of the formal rules of our first language. But this is the paradox of psychoanalysis; we only know clearly what we originally failed to comprehend, having been forced to repeatedly act it out until we could consciously re-cognize the experience for what it really is.

Furthermore, we see in the work of Outsiders that they 'naturally' adopt the techniques Freud himself came to employ in the treatment of unconscious symptoms; symptoms produced by the unrecognized experiences' trying to make themselves known to consciousness:

1) They repeat or reiterate the problematic experience *ad nauseum*.

2) They adhere rigidly to rules, not because these in themselves have meaning, but because any set of limits, if strictly conformed to, appears to facilitate the revelation of underlying hidden structures. Note however, that it is the continuous reiteration of these rules which enables the pattern to be revealed, not the rules themselves.

3) They do not decide in advance what they wish to represent, they let the image grow out of itself; ie, they do not censor, but allow a free play of associations. Again, it is not a predetermination which governs the overall composition, but something that is revealed only through the repetition.

4) Everything is regarded as significant: no element is seen as meaningless, therefore no element is regarded as either accidental or wrong. The starting point for many such composers is often a ready-made spot or mark in which is seen a fragment of an event that is then elaborated to its fullness by the composer. (Again, this echoes analytic technique where the client interjects some feature of the analyst or their sur-

roundings that they regard as significant, then proceeds to construct a whole picture from this.)

5) Though the making of a composition is definitively a process of working-through, it has no other aim than itself; ie, it is not the finished work that is of import, but the process of recreation, of remembering through repeatedly acting-out, itself.

All these techniques are consciously employed by both outsider artists and by psychoanalysts in the clinic, when helping analyzands liberate their forgotten or mis-re-cognized experiences, ie, the gaps in consciousness that come to constitute the otherness of the un-conscious. The question is whether these re-creative techniques can also be used consciously by non-outsiders in the construction of their compositions, be these visual or verbal?

Leaving aside the issue of the personal therapeutic value such practices might have, the importance of this question lies in the fact that it bears on the general problem of langue, ie, on whether our culturally developed descriptive systems are adequate or not to the representation of our underlying cognitive experiences, especially the experience of our being-in-language?

It is today generally held to be the case that they are not, for, as Lacan, drawing on the work of Kurt Godel, so clearly articulates, there is a point where every descriptive system must fail. What is open to dispute however is whether the precise point of such an inadequacy is absolute or contingent, ie, whether the particular point at which a particular langue fails is the point at which all other langues must also fail. It is one of the great mistakes of modern theories of representation, be these purely linguistic or whether they also take into account the fact of language's being inhabited by a psychic subject, that they tend to project onto the rest of the universe the precise point of their own incapacity or impotentiality.

The support for this projection is the mathematician Kurt Godel's proof that every formal system adequate for the representation of number theory is by definition capable of producing statements whose status is, from the perspective of the system itself, undecidable. That is, all such systems contain statements which exhibit the limits of the system itself, and hence point to at least the possibility of a wider or more general system of representation. But Godel merely proved that every such system must have some such point. He did not say that this point is the same for every system. Indeed, a moment's thought is enough to convince us that this cannot be the case, for different systems are composed of different kinds of signs, and hence they cannot all possibly fail in the same way. To say therefore that every system fails at the point where it recognizes there is some-thing it cannot say clearly, is not the same as to say that each fails to say the same thing.

But this is a very general point. What is of more interest to us is the specific question of our own systems, ie, where do they really fail? For, as shown above, it is simply not the case that the inherent point of failure in our visual langues is the point at which they are called upon to represent the experience of being-in-space.

It is only so long as we continue to conceptualize this as the experience of the absence of (some other) 'things' that we experience this point as being coincidental with the limit of our representational systems. As the Outsiders so articulately show, once we re-conceptualize space as a tangible presence in its own right, we find that it is perfectly representable, and hence not at the limit of our representational systems. What they thus show is that, though there must be some limit to the representational capacities of our langues, this limit does not lie at the point where these langues are called upon to represent space.

One of the consequences of Godel's theorem seems to be that the modern world has wholeheartedly, even luxuriously, succumbed to the general principle of the undecidable or unrepresentable, and quickly moved to lumping everything difficult into that basket. It would not, perhaps, be too inaccurate to state that articulating the unrepresentable has become the fetish of modern intellectuals, and also, sadly, of many artists. By being much more careful in the analysis of their own experiences Outsider artists show that it is possible to be much more precise in distinguishing between the representable and the unrepresentable. By constantly re-enacting the gaps in their own knowledge through juxtaposing these with the experiences they are conscious of these special subjects show that, while our langues must, by definition, be limited, they are not quite so limited as we might like to imagine.

Without wishing to propose that we return to an unreflective positivism, perhaps it would not be too much to suggest that, with a little more of this kind of analysis, and a little less devotion to post-modern impotence, we too might find we have the capacity to say many things we have so far assumed to be unsayable. Of all the experiences awaiting such a recreative resurrection, the experience of being-in-space is one most surely in need of this analysis.

Glossary

The definitions of the new senses expressed in the terms of the following glossary should not be deemed exhaustive, but rather as starting points for a richer appreciation of the immensity of sense contained in this superb linguistic organism called 'English'.

Being-incorporated: The state of being embodied in some 'matter'. This matter may be physical, as when Being is incarnated in flesh, or 'mental', as when Being is manifest in language, for language is also a matter which must become manifestly embodied to acquire 'existence' in a concrete manner.

Being-in-|tself: Being without embodiment, Being which 'is', but is in some way not (yet) manifest. The question of what such a phenomenon may be is very complex. It may even be that there is no unembodied mode of Being. The point is to recognise that Being is not confined to pure existence, especially of the physical kind, ie, not confined to Being-incarnate-(d).

Being-in-Language: The mode of Being which is manifested or incorporated in language. What is at stake here is the 'body of language'.

Being-present: May be opposed to Being-absent. May also be opposed to Being-represent-(ed). Though it may be that both these can be manifest simultaneously with Being-present.

|'s: Here the - 's' - may be seen to have either the sense of the verb – to be – or of the possessive case, and the I may be interpreted as I, one, or eye. The intersection of I, one and eye is not accidental, even if this is not apparent in any other language. Thus we get: I is: I's: One is: One's: eyes: (the) eye is, etc.

Key words: repetition . space

|'s-self: As above for the - I's - component, with the sense of selfhood added.

Matter's: The - 's' - as above. Thus, the phrase 'what matter's' read as what matter is, what matter possesses, or even, what is possessed by matter.

Mis-re-cognition: A false recognition. See below.

Playin': Here the playing is seen as a plane and also as plain.

Pre-sense or Presense: This shows that what is called 'presence' is actually a mode of Being which comes *before sense*.

Re-cognise and Re-cognition: To recognise is to cognise or make sense *again*.

Re-creation and Re-creativity: Recreation is the state of creating *again*. In the case of art, this may be differentiated from the mode of 'original' creation, that is, *creation ex nihilo*, for recreation is a mode of copying, remaking, or even of representation.

Re-mark: To remark (upon) something is to mark it *again*.

Re-member: To remember is a form of re-organisation or re-embodiment. What we remember is a mode of reorganising our sense, either of ourselves or some body other. It is a mode of organising (some body) *again*.

Re-presense or Represense: To represent (some thing or some I) is to present, or pre-sense, (it) *again*.

'Space or 'S-pace: The - 's' - as above. Thus, 'space' is both a mode of Being and a mode of Being-possessed. When a hyphen is inserted in this space, it is seen as a mode of Being-at-peace or of Being-possessed-by-a-(sense-of)-peace.

SEINE

Jack Vanarsky/Ou. Pein. Po.

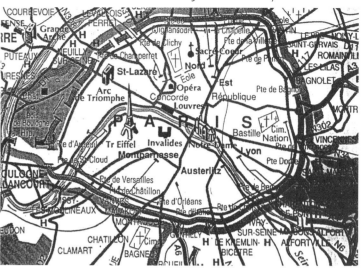

Project for the realignment of the Seine as it crosses Paris, 1991 (bicentennial of Baron Haussmann). Presented at the *Attenzione al Potenziale* exhibition, Florence, May, 1991, and at the *Visions Urbaines* exhibition, Centre Georges Pompidou, Paris, February, 1994.

To rectify the course of the Seine so that it runs at right angles to the axis of the boulevard Saint-Michel/boulevard de Strasbourg:

(1) Take a large number of identical plans of Paris.
(2) Make a straight cut along the axis, keep the left or right hand side of the plan. For each of the remaining plans make similar cuts parallel to the axis, each cut a few millimetres away from the last. Keep the left or the right hand side of each plan. When finished superimpose the pieces to reconstitute the plan of Paris.
(3) Modify the angle of each visible fragment of the Seine to establish a straight line.

Consequences

Direct: The realignment of the Seine creates a grand axis for quick transportation by river, it results in a magnificent perspective of the bridges of Paris.

Complementary: Paris is re-balanced, the Left Bank achieves equality with the Right Bank.

Concomitant: The Bois de Boulogne is projected into the centre of Paris, creating a vast green space in the heart of the capital. A new urban tissue is generated, pre-Haussman in type, with many lanes and cul-de-sacs, a picturesque quality which compensates for the rigour of the river axis. A number of monuments disappear, others multiply. For example l'Opéra de Garnier, Sacre Cœur and l'Arc de Triomphe go while Les Invalides, Le Cimetière de Montparnasse, le Centre George Pompidou and l'Opéra de la Bastille are doubled. The suburbs penetrate the city.

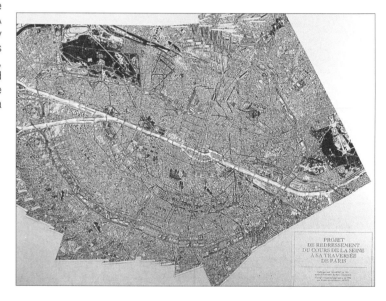

Key words : cut . flux . flow

SHADOWTOWN

MVRDV

The old centre of Bergen op Zoom is protected by the Dutch Monument Act. It defines that new buildings should be erected in an 'invisible' way, within the protected zone, in order to maintain the character of the old town. By projecting all possible view lines from the old town, over the planning zone around the central railway station of the town, the potential envelope can contain the building production in the Bergen op Zoom region for the coming twenty years! It makes it imaginable that the forests, pastoral hills and bay can be safeguarded from the sprawl of houses, offices and small factories. This envelope manifests itself as a 'mountain' of potential mass in the shadow of the 'eternal idyll' of Bergen op Zoom. Urbanism can thus be defined as a 'datascape' of potentials. [Urban Development in Bergen op Zoom; Credit – Winy Maas, Jacob van Rijs, Nathalie de Vries, Frans Blok; client – Stichting Probleem Pleinen Prijsvraag, Roosendaal; project – competition design 1993]

Key words : ghost . indistinct

SHOGAWA

Carlos Villanueva-Brandt

The building is made up of different parts and routes which allow disparate individual views and experiences of the park, mountain, river and landscape. As an object the building acts as a composite pavilion and a gateway to the park as a whole and can be divided into three parts; main, video and frame.

These three parts do not sit in isolation, but are complemented by the contoured seating, the proposed path from the museums and the ceremonial steps. The main part sits like an island in the moat, highlighting the importance of water to the site and contains three contrasting levels that form the pavilion. These levels vary both in material and their relationship to the surrounding river, park and landscape.

The lowest level represents Shogawa as a whole being filled with gravel and dissected by a stream; the running water relates to the river and the side walls are analogous to the existing dams. The second level, constructed from timber and steel, is suspended within the main volume and provides multiple views and a sense of suspension within the landscape. Level three, which is the roof of the main part, is simply delineated by the canopy structure and four free-standing planes of glass expressing the geometry of the building whilst also allowing for a full awareness of the landscape.

In the video part again there are three levels, but the views are more restricted and particular than in the main part; the real views of the landscape complemented by the views of the video screens. The screens, which are placed on levels one and two, transmit images from inaccessible points within the park, river and mountain.

The frame element provides the uppermost level and, unlike the other two parts, addresses the river axis providing views along the river towards the two dams. With their contrasts and relationships, the three parts of the building provide a varied sequence of spaces, edited sets of views of the landscape and most importantly a deeper understanding of Shogawa and its surroundings.

Key words : according to the form . simulate . territory

SPAGHETTI FINGERS

Robert Lawson

Linear scanning imaging is a photographic method capable of generating infinitely overlapping partial images, then fusing them together in a single image – a process of deconstruction coupled with reconstruction. A three-dimensional reality is translated into a two-dimensional image via a one-dimensional information field. Linear scanning transformations occur when there is relative motion between the film plane, the scanning line of image formation and the subject. These transformations are not optical distortions as portions of the subject not in motion are rendered in their 'normal', static form. Every linear scanning image, like the annual rings of a tree, or the layers of sedimentary rock, describes a chronology. A systematic progression of time is presented across the image.

Key words : deception . distortion

88

STEREOTOMIC PERMUTATIONS

Preston Scott Cohen

Architectural form is always paradoxical. It remains estranged and autonomous because it escapes the cultural categories by which it is assimilated and situated. The programmes that necessitate, and the materials that give body to form, are also protagonists in the struggle against its self-determinacy and autonomy. With regard to the demand for it to be categorized, form is instigative and reactive; autonomy thrives on contestation. Accordingly, the formally autonomous project of architecture continually reasserts and transgresses its authoritative paradigms of argumentation and reconfiguration.

Evidence that architectural form is able to operate with legibility is an indispensable invitation to decipherment; to the paradoxical autonomy of architecture. Because so few linguistic formal conventions continue to be sustained in architectural culture, it is becoming increasingly difficult to identify paradigmatic operations susceptible to transgression. One could begin by distorting configurations of symmetry, seriality, linearity and progression, by subjecting them to scale, elasticity and intersection – operations that continue to resist discrete identification while remaining recognizable. It could be argued, however, that the exponents of paradox in architecture are not only configurative but also inscriptive. One such instigator can be found among the conflicts and synonymies of perspectival and stereotomic techniques of projection. This is where the project 'Stereotomic Permutations' begins.

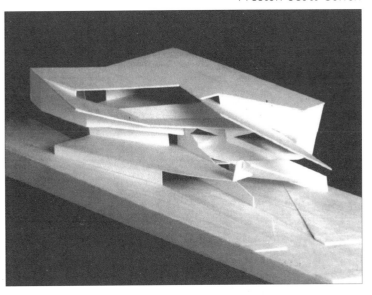

Perspective and orthography are instrumental to a discipline that produces artifacts that are not self-identical with their medium. Is it possible for the disparity between drawings and buildings to correlate with the discrepancy between paradigms and their distortions? In 'Stereotomic Permutations', opposing systems of projection are peculiarly combined in order to become techniques of formal transgression. The distance point method of perspective projection introduces a distortion of symmetrical and serial operations and configurations; stereotomy is deployed to refute the categorical distinctions between perspective and orthography.

The distance point method constructs a volatile symmetry by requiring that the perspective be reversed in relation to its object across a measuring line. The result is a set of similar configurations (an orthographic object and a perspectival object) that differ proportionally and dimensionally. Conventionally, the measuring line defines and holds apart the opposing methods of representation: the convergence and illusionism of perspective versus the parallelism and actual dimensions of orthographics. In this project, the implicit symmetrical order is repeatedly brought to bear on its objects and perspectives by forcing them to intersect, join and fold back on themselves to form a series.

When the lineaments of a perspective are brought into coincidence with those of stereotomic projection, fixity of point of view and the infinity of orthography become mired in a logical contradiction. On the one hand, points of convergence (the eye and distance point) constellate a perspective and an object. On the other hand, these same points, extended as fold lines, are shared by the surfaces of three-dimensional objects formed by both the original object and its perspective; since they are stereotomic, these combinatory objects contradict perspective by positioning the viewer at an immeasurable distance from the entire object. The result is an apparent anamorphosis, with the points from where one could gain an undistorted view in positions that can never be occupied.

In these investigations, reversals exaggerate the combined methods and in so doing eliminate the boundary between description and perception. The matrix that once served to separate has become the process by which wholes are rendered indivisible.

ABOVE: Anamorphic compression; CENTRE AND BELOW: Prado

Key words : deviation . distortion . repetition

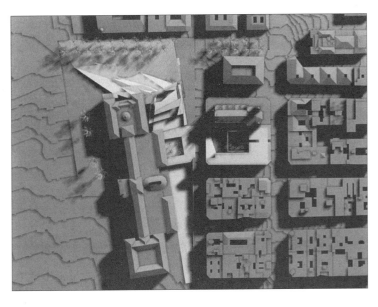

STOREFRONT WALL MACHINE

Vito Acconci/Steven Holl

The site is: a narrow triangular space that serves as an alternative gallery for architecture and art.

The programme is: an artist/architect collaboration that results in a new façade for the gallery.

The project is: an adjustable and variable façade, a usable wall.

The wall is: white-painted plaster inside, and supra-board (a concrete-like panel) outside.

The façade is: designed so that it can be adjusted variously for different exhibitions, according to the particular needs of each exhibitor.

The wall is divided into segments. Vertical seams separate the wall into panels that pivot, like revolving doors, side to side; the pivoting wall-panels can be secured at various points – at different angles to the fixed wall – a wall-panel can be turned inside out. Horizontal seams separate the wall into panels that pivot like louvres, up and down; the higher panels function as windows – open to different degrees – the lower panels can be turned and fixed at right angles to the wall, so that they function as tables and benches.

When all the panels are rotated, there's continuity between inside and outside: the gallery becomes part of the street, and the street becomes part of the sidewalk. The wall is an instrument to be used (turned and sat on, stepped through) in the middle of a continuous space, with no inside or outside.

When all the panels are pulled shut, flush with the fixed wall, light from the inside seeps outside, through the seams, and vice versa. The closed panels can be arranged in any one of three eventualities: supra-board, so that the gallery presents itself shut off, like a fortress; white plaster, so that the gallery is turned inside-out, or a mix of grey supra-board and white plaster, a patchwork of inside and outside on a single surface.
[Storefront For Art And Architecture, New York, 1993 (Acconci Studio: Luis Vera, design & engineering; Steven Holl): Materials – Supra-board, plaster, steel, hinges]

Key words : closure/non-closure . continue . plane . play a role

SUBDIVISIONS

a. topos/Jane Harrison

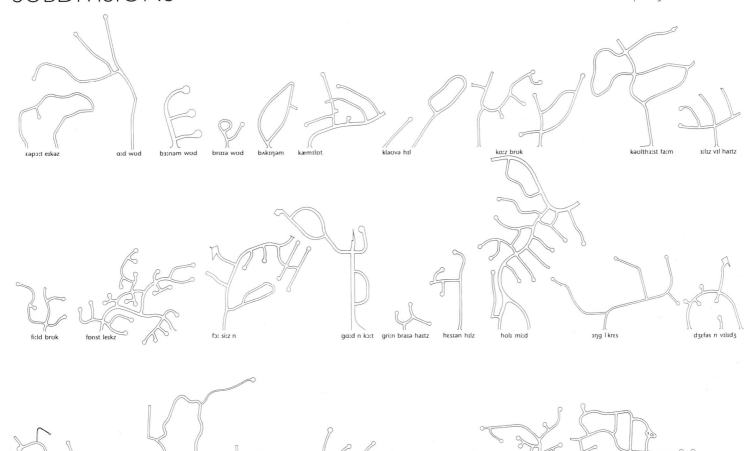

ɛəpɔːt eɪkəz   ɑːd wʊd   bɜːnəm wʊd   brɑɪə wʊd   bʌkɪŋəm   kæmɪlɒt   klaʊvə hɪl   kɑːz brʊk   kaʊlthɜːst faːm   ɜːlɪz vɪl haɪts

fiːld brʊk   fɒrɪst leɪkz   fɔː siːz n   gaːd n kɔːt   griːn braɪə haɪts   hɛsɪən hɪlz   holɪ miːd   ɪŋ l krɛs   dʒɛfəs n vɪlɪdʒ

mɒnt vjuː   aʊk fɒrɪst   ʃɜːwʊd faːmz   rɪo haɪts   tɪrɪ brʊk   vɪlɪdʒ skwɛˊ   wɪlˊʊbiː   wɪlˊʊ leɪk   wʊd brʊk   wɪn rɪdʒ

Sample from a project reassessing the American suburban landscape. The focus of the study is the area around the US Route 29 as it passes through Albermale County in Virginia. This area was selected because the transition from farmland to suburb is in its early stages. The strategies adopted by landowners and developers in setting out subdivisions, the ordinances that apply, marketing and naming policies can be explored in a very direct way.
This is an examination of FICTIONS of SAFETY and the devices, including artificial memory and nostalgia, as well as plans that negotiate independence, communality; seclusion, exposure; and proximity, distance that are deployed in the construction of these 'fictions'.

Key words: algorithms . ordinary . repetition . un-forget

TABLE T

A₃

Field + Glyphs = Tablet, Table, Tabula

[A] Abandoned – not plumbing depths but rather joyfully exploring an excessive horizontal network of transmissions and mediations, discovering surfaces of inclusion, negotiating an overabundance of connection which paradoxically reveals, simultaneously, a surplus of dead ends.

[B] Banished
Out: depth – In: surface
Out: archeological insight – In: a game of hide and seek
Out: knowledge – In: uncertainty, speculation and make-believe
Out: direct encounters with the past – In: a Chinese puzzle

[C] Chinese puzzle – an intersection of pedagogy, free experimentation and recall, understood not as memory but as a private or shared hallucination, as alternate realities, multiple realities or fake reality.

Example: begun in 1968 and still in progress, Armand Schwerner's 'Tablets'. The tablets (scholarly translations) do not observe any scholarly convention: the (scholar/translator's) annotations are often idiosyncratic, and the identity of the scholar/translator is concealed.
Conversation with Willard Gingerich (Summer 1993): Gingerich suggests the most interesting parts are those that the scholar/translator makes as a commentary on his labour. Schwerner replies:
Well, he (the scholar/translator) has three generally identifiable self-presentations in the last two tablets and the one that I am working on now. That is, the subtitles of the late tablets are: 'The Laboratory'; 'Teaching'; 'Memoirs of the Scholar/Translator'. So what we're talking about now is your bent towards the memoirs aspect of the scholar/translator. His overt bent is toward the laboratory aspect. And he is seized by, almost, it appears, in spite of himself, the teaching aspect of his own preaching, which he would I think disallow immediately.

Key words : glyphs . impersonate . word play

TABLES

Armand Schwerner

- A Tablet?:   chant of nonsense syllables, transliterated. The Tablet people liked 'nonsense'.
- A Tablet?:   layers like the J and H etc variant sources of the OT books thru *Joshua*.
- A Tablet?:   The verb is time-past etc and conceptual. Its absence to add a nominal immediacy.
- A Tablet: The Rohrscach idea.
- The Tablet of Shapes
- The Tablet of the child's power to change himself into whatever.
- One Tablet completely [   ]!
- The Tablets: Animism: who is walking? what is it in the self that talks? is there a self-envelope for what talks?
- The Tablet of Peripheries
- The Tablet of Dissidence (Lautreamont)
- The Tablet of Great Dissidence
- What is 'I' ?
- In the Tablets, how does one individual man come across? how's his psyche / context?
        like 'is the man a bird?'
            'is the man four-legged and with teeth?'
            'is the man a tree?'
- A berdache Tablet
- Man in the beginnings of his being forked in 2 on the 2-halved Tablet: but not sure the parts are correctly put together.
- Animals Tablet: translation troubles
- The Tablets: formal games and invention give rise to substantive concerns and social reality.
- The scholar-translator himself has different moods, heightenings
- Really fantastic: the sequence from hieroglyph, cuneiform, syllabary, alphabet . . . relativity of all things to the imaginative makings. Zones. Texts of the 'future' – 'Science-fiction' of the past confounding temporality. Who is speaking?

[Extract from 'Tablets Journals/Divaginations', postscript to *Tablets I-XXVI*, Armand Schwerner, Atlas Press, London, 1989]

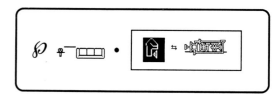

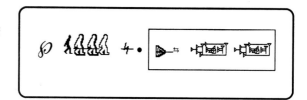

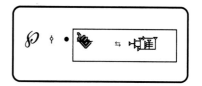

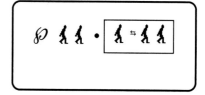

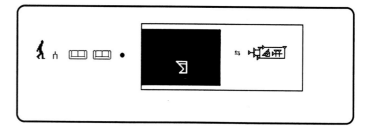

Key words: glyphs . field

WORLD:

A$_4$

In the early 1960s, Constantinos A Doxiadis envisaged an 'Ecumenopolis' which would consist of major cities linked to each other by air traffic and electronic communications more firmly than to the surrounding districts of the countries in which they are located. A global élite, crossing national boundaries daily, would be the ultimate form of civilisation. According to Metabolist theory set out by Kisho Kurokawa in 1967, each of these cities would be a 'Metapolis', a junction point of mobile information built in 'Super-Architecture'.

In 1996 it has become clear that these predictions have become facts: future shock is no longer shocking, merely normal; jet lag is no longer worth discussing as it has become permanent, and play time has become an imperative as the relentless machine of urban development grinds on. With hundreds of entirely new cities planned or under construction in mainland China, and the South East Asian nations racing through accelerated building programs to attract the wealthy, but disenfranchised or disenchanted from, Hong Kong, the risk takers from Taiwan and manufacturers from Korea, the 'Super-City' has become a reality. Apparently constructed from nothing, the Metapolis has unprec-

edented density, is built at unimaginable speed, deals with huge quantities of information and reconciles complex cultural differences whilst producing history and wealth and challenging conceptions of democracy and individual freedom as alternative forms of agreement are theorised and tested in Singapore, the Philippines and Indonesia. The character of the Metapolis, the global production site where the boundary between what is real and what is simulated is increasingly vague, demands the abandonment of certainty and the acceptance of continuous change, fluidity and flux. History is articulated in relation to the future and not the past, judgement is suspended and Winnicott's question 'did you find it in the world or did you make it up?' is resolutely put out of play.

Key words : across form . lands . play . territory

AZ . . .

Jane Harrison/David Turnbull

(continued from page 8)

. . . In Helsinki, the project for **Arabianranta** (pp11-14) uses a game structure to involve multiple, large constituencies and individual interests in a condition of both perpetual conflict and mutual tolerance to produce unprecedented possibilities, addressing serious issues. The game board is the public space of negotiation which allows the local implications of globalisation and ecological concerns to be reframed. Play negotiates stability and instability and demands participation. The Paris **Goose Game** (pp36-38) involves fifty architect/players from Europe and the USA. The architectural projects themselves are not as important as the game which has become an effective device for attracting public attention and provoking changes in policy. The **Quadratura** project (pp67-70) extends an imaginary surface, a ceiling, across Cambridge, England. Above the ceiling there is a space without regulation, a kind of 'heaven'. The occupants of buildings that are cut by the 'ceiling' are designated 'angels'. This project liberatingly draws fantasy space and legal space together. Project **Row Houses** (pp76-77) begins with buildings that are about to be thrown away, condemned. This project is not about transgression, it is not about the new, but it is about dreamspace and recall, it is also about collective action that powerfully mobilises corporate support, rather than fighting against it, to create new social spaces. **Negotiation** (pp60-61) is a negotiation, with the new structures of Minato Mirai, an ubiquitous post-Metabolist city, a page from the encyclopedic *S,M,L,XL* (010, Rotterdam, 1996), a negotiation between Rem Koolhaas and Bruce Mau; the project and the page, on the page, as a field of glyphs.

Bastille (p15) is both a monument and a playground, an urban icon which is actually dismantled so that it can be re-formed in the mind, the material concentration of the thing is dissolved as it is materialised as a thought. **Bottles** (p15), **Chaos** (p17) and **Micro-Macro** (pp53-55) draw out the complexity that is already in the world, either by making rearrangements of surplus materials of incredible beauty, or probing the microscopic intricacies of natural processes in a state that is 'far from equilibrium'. **Bricks** (p16) is a real carton, problematising authenticity. **Opera** (pp 62-64) redefines the public building as infrastructure, investigating the *new* potential in old structural principles. **Klapper Hall** (p45) and **Storefront** (p92) are both 'public' projects.

In 1960 Raymond Queneau and Francois Le Lionnais formed the Oulipo, *Ouvroir de Literature Potentielle*, an association of writers and mathematicians devoted to the project of incorporating mathematics into literary creation. The members of the Oulipo are interested in artificial restrictions and rigorously applied procedures which they see as potentiality, not limitation. Membership is decided by election and has included: Italo Calvino, Francois Le Lionnais, Harry Mathews, Georges Perec, Raymond Queneau and Jacques Roubaud among 29 members over 35 years. Affiliated with the Oulipo are a number of groups who explore the same issues in relation to other disciplines. We have selected work by members of Ou.Pho.Po. and Ou.Pein.Po. dealing with photography and painting respectively, as having a clear and explicit bearing on architecture; **Bruges-La-Morte** (p16), **Les Halles** (p46), the **Morpholo** (pp57-59) and **Seine** (p84) all work with the psychic, erotic or morphological potential of procedures with prestated parameters. Each project is infused with a sly humour which discovers the subversive in the rule, the unexpected possibility in the convention.

Interruptions (p45) and **Spaghetti Fingers** (p88) are concerned with the spatial and formal implications of the interplay of a mechanical rule driven procedure and random, manual intervention. The interruptions are constructed without an object, where procedure + light = field. The production of the *invisible*, high density development of **Shadowtown** (p84) could be described as the result of the equation: line of sight/non sight + procedure = field of maximum potential. **City** (p17) addresses the anxiety that what is in the computer, dimensionally correct and precisely specified, is as real as what is outside. In the way that psychic remote viewers used by the CIA during the Cold War could 'visit' sites that could not be penetrated in any other way, the viewer enters the computer city through the screen, depthless space becomes thickly material.

A field of television monitors and cameras displaces and repositions remote views of the natural surroundings of **Shogawa** (pp86-88) in relation to views framed by the building structure, recalling other gateways, views of history. You are where you are and where you are not, spatially and temporally. **Disturbed Sur Realism** (p21) explores the qualities of computer manipulated images that are no longer either photographs or montages. The interplay of the **Light Ness** (pp51-52) of data and **Heavy Ness** (pp39-42) of matter, as Italo Calvino suggests in *Six Memos for the Next Millennium* (Vintage, 1993, p5) is not straightforward: 'Medusa's blood gives birth to a winged horse, Pegasus – the heaviness of stone is transformed into it opposite'.

Arakawa and Madeline Gins' first House of Reversible Destiny, **Gifu** (pp27-34) has now been built and occupied by thousands of visitors. For them 'the game both begins and is over or transmutes into a non-game once the regional approaches to (the securing of a) reversible destiny have been determined'.

CONTRIBUTORS

a.topos, London-based international architectural group, formed in 1990 by **Jane Harrison** and **David Turnbull** – Diploma Unit Masters, Architectural Association, London. **Vito Acconci** (with the Acconci Studio: Luis Vera, Janny Scrider, Charles Doherty), New York artist working with architecture and landscape. **Stan Allen**, New York-based architect and Assistant Professor of Architecture at Columbia University. **Edward Allington**, British artist represented by the Lisson Gallery. **APCY Architects**, London-based practice formed by Paola Yacoub and Alain Chiaradia in 1993. **Arakawa and Madeline Gins**, New York-based artists, exhibited internationally. A show devoted to their work will open at the Guggenheim later this year. **Baratloo-Balch Architects**, New York-based architectural practice formed in 1984 by Mojdeh Baratloo and Clifton Balch. **Beevor Mull Architects**, British-based practice formed in 1986 by Catrina Beevor and Robert Mull (co-founder of the NATO group in 1983 and Diploma Unit Master at the Architectural Association, London). **Jennifer Bloomer**, American architect, academic and writer. **Jae-Eun Choi**, Korean artist based in Japan. **Chora**, a London-based research institute for urban studies established by Raoul Bunschoten. **Preston Scott Cohen**, Boston-based architect and Assistant Professor at the GSD, Harvard. **dECOi**, Paris-based architectural group established in 1991 by Mark Goulthorpe, Zainie Zainul and Yee Pin Tan. **Elizabeth Diller and Richardo Scofidio**, New York-based artists/architects. **Harris Dimitropoulos**, Atlanta-based architect/artist. **Paul Edwards**, Paris-based photographer and member of Ou.Pho.Po. **Joan Fontcuberta**, Barcelona-based photographer, represented by the Virginia Zabrieski Gallery, New York. **Thieri Foulc**, Paris-based artist and mathematician, member of the Collège de 'Pataphysique and later Ou.Pein.Po. **Frank O Gehry**, American architect, principal of Frank O Gehry and Associates, Los Angeles. **Heidi Gilpin**, Los Angeles-based writer and academic, dramaturge for the Frankfurt Ballet. **Philip Johnson**, American

architect. **Rem Koolhaas**, author of *Delirious New York*, principal of the Office of Metropolitan Architecture, Rotterdam. **Sanford Kwinter**, American academic and theorist, co-editor of *Zone*. **Robert Lawson**, American photographer. **Jean-Jacques Lecercle**, writer and theorist, Professor of English at the University of Paris, Nanterre. **Rick Lowe** Houston-based African-American artist. **Liquid Inc**, Atlanta-based architectural/art practice formed by Amy Landesberg and Lisa Quatrale. **Alison Mark**, writer and academic living in London. **Bruce Mau**, designer of *Zone*, principal of the design firm BMD. **Matt Mullican**, New York-based artist, represented by Barbara Gladstone Gallery, New York. **MVRDV**, Amsterdam-based architectural practice formed in 1991 by Winy Maas, Jacob van Rijs and Natalie de Vries. **Project Row Houses**, Houston-based art and cultural community centre founded by Rick Lowe. **RAAUm**, architectural collaboration of Jesse Reiser, Stan Allen, Polly Apfelbaum and Nanako Umemoto. **Reiser and Umemoto**, New York-based architecture practice formed by Jesse Reiser and Nanako Umemoto. **Claire Robinson**, Rhode Island-based architect and teacher, co-ordinator of Archi XX, Paris. **Dieter Roth**, Swiss born artist/writer, collaborator in Daniel Spoerri's *An Anecdoted Topography of Chance*. **Jerome Sans**, art critic and independent curator who has written extensively for contemporary art journals in Europe and the United States. **Armand Schwerner**, American poet and teacher. **Jack Vanarsky**, Paris-based artist and member of Ou.Pein.Po. **Carlos Villanueva-Brandt**, London-based architect, co-founder of the NATO group in 1983, and Diploma Unit Master at the Architectural Association, London. **Paul Virilio**, writer and urbanist, director of the Ecole Spéciale d'Architecture, Paris. **VSBA**, Robert Venturi, Denise Scott Brown and Associates Architects, Philadelphia. **Christine Wertheim**, London-based philosopher and critical theorist. **James Williamson**, Boston-based architect and Assistant Professor at the GSD, Harvard University.